Strategies for Sustaining Digital Libraries

Copyright © 2008

This collection is covered by the following Creative Commons License.

Attribution-NonCommercial-NoDerivs 3.0 License

You are free to copy, distribute, and display this work under the following conditions:

(BY:)	**Attribution.** You must attribute the work in the manner specified by the author or licensor (but not in any way that suggests that they endorse you or your use of the work). Specifically, you must state that the work was originally published in *Strategies for Sustaining Digital Libraries* (2008), Katherine Skinner and Martin Halbert, Eds. and you must attribute the author(s).
(⊘)	**Noncommercial.** You may not use this work for commercial purposes.
(=)	**No Derivative Works.** You may not alter, transform, or build upon this work.

For any reuse or distribution, you must make clear to others the license terms of this work.

Any of these conditions can be waived if you get permission from the copyright holder.

Nothing in this license impairs or restricts the author's moral rights.

The above is a summary of the full license, which is available at the following URL:

> http://creativecommons.org/licenses/by-nc-nd/3.0/legalcode

Publication and Cataloging Information:

ISBN: 0-9772994-1-4

Editors: Katherine Skinner, Martin Halbert
Copy Editors: Mary Battle

Publisher: Emory University
Digital Library Publications
Atlanta, GA 30322

TABLE OF CONTENTS

List of Tables and Figures iv

Acknowledgements v

Sustaining Digital Libraries: An Introduction (Martin Halbert and Katherine Skinner, Emory University) 3

Once in a Hundred Generations (Paul Arthur Berkman, University of California, Santa Barbara) 11

Digital Sustainability: Weaving a Tapestry of Interdependency to Advance Digital Library Programs (Tyler O. Walters, Georgia Institute of Technology) 22

What Is This New Devilry? Digital Libraries and the Fate of Faculty Scholarship and Publishing (Bradley Daigle, University of Virginia) 41

Sustainability, Publishing, and Digital Libraries (Michael Furlough, Penn State University Libraries) 59

Principles and Activities of Digital Curation for Developing Successful and Sustainable Repositories (Leslie Johnston, University of Virginia) 84

When the Music's Over (Mary Marlino, Tamara Sumner, Karon Kelly, and Michael Wright, University Corporation for Atmospheric Research, University of Colorado at Boulder) 97

About the Editors and Contributors 112

LIST OF TABLES AND FIGURES

Tables

1.1 Sustainability Elements of Digital Information Organizations 16
1.2 Matrix of "Sustainability Vignettes" 18

Figures

1.1 Human Communication Eras..12
1.2 Borromean Rings of Meaning 14
1.3 NSDL Funding..17
2.1 Digital Sustainability Model 28
2.2 Digital Sustainability Model as Applied to MetaArchive.....................................37
3.1 Model of a Digital Library Environment 53
6.1 Digital Library for Earth System Education (DLESE) site 99

ACKNOWLEDGEMENTS

This book was inspired by the Andrew W. Mellon and Robert W. Woodruff Library sponsored symposium *Sustaining Digital Libraries* held at Emory University in the summer of 2006. We wish to begin by thanking all of the planners, implementers, presenters, and attendees who helped to make the *Sustaining Digital Libraries Symposium* a success.

Our appreciation also goes to the institutions and departments that provided various kinds of support to enable this symposium, including the Andrew W. Mellon Foundation, which provided financial support for the event, and Emory University's Robert W. Woodruff Library, which provided the overall framework of support and the facilities for the conference. We are also grateful to Rick Luce, Emory University Vice Provost and Director of Libraries, who both supported and contributed to this event.

The conversations that began at the symposium have carried forward, in many cases becoming part of this collection of essays. We would like to thank all of the contributors to this volume, first for their work in creating and supporting various digital libraries across the humanities, social sciences, and sciences; and second for their contributions to the intellectual substance of this book.

Finally, we would like to extend a special thanks to those staff members of the Digital Programs and Systems division who worked on both the symposium and the manuscript, including Erika Farr, Robin Conner, Sarah Toton, and Mary Battle. As we've said before, it often takes a community to write a book, and our community has been one of support, encouragement, and often great ideas – something we do not take for granted for even a moment!

Katherine Skinner, Martin Halbert
Atlanta, Georgia
February 2008

Strategies for Sustaining Digital Libraries

Edited by Katherine Skinner and Martin Halbert

Emory University
Digital Library Publications
Atlanta, Georgia

Sustaining Digital Libraries: An Introduction

Katherine Skinner (Emory University)
Martin Halbert (Emory University)

Abstract: Outlines the themes and contributions of *Strategies for Sustaining Digital Libraries* and offers summary conclusions about the core topics discussed.

We are at the inception of a new field – that of digital librarianship. Given that this is an emerging field and that so much is changing within our underlying infrastructure, how can leaders begin talking about, planning for, and implementing strategies for sustaining digital libraries as they become essential sources of knowledge?

It is these questions that have led us to produce *Strategies for Sustaining Digital Libraries*. This collection of essays is a report of early findings from pioneers who have worked to establish digital libraries, not merely as experimental projects, but as ongoing services and collections intended to be sustained over time in ways consistent with the long held practices of print-based libraries. Particularly during this period of extreme technological transition, it is imperative that programs across the nation – and indeed the world – actively share their innovations, experiences, and techniques in order to begin cultivating new isomorphic, or commonly held, practices. The collective sentiment of the field is that we must begin to transition from a punctuated, project-based mode of advancing innovative information services to an ongoing programmatic mode of sustaining digital libraries for the long haul.

This collection of essays began with discussions at a symposium entitled *Sustaining Digital Libraries* held at Emory University on October 6, 2006. Conversations at this symposium highlighted the need for a book to capture findings, observations, insights, and advice on this topic, leading the organizers of the event to champion the creation of this collection. This volume resulted in part from the dialogue that ensued between experienced leaders of digital libraries as they explored the most promising models for sustaining such efforts in the long term.

In the first portion of this introductory essay we will review the scope of the problem, outline the contributions found in this monograph, and then offer summary conclusions on the topic.

DIGITAL LIBRARIES AND THE EXPANDING UNIVERSE OF RESEARCH INFORMATION

We take a very broad definitional view of this topic, contending that all of the myriad networked information resources now used by scholars (researchers, teachers, and graduate students) should fundamentally be understood as digital libraries. Such resources must be sustained over generations in order to support the long-term needs of scholars for research and citation. But the pace and scale of the production of new digital resources makes this a challenging prospect.

A bit of framing context is useful at this point. According to the "Expanding Digital Universe: A Forecast of Worldwide Information Growth Through 2010" study by the IDC and EMC (2007), the world created upwards of 161 exabytes (161 *billion* gigabytes) of information in 2006. In isolation, that number is virtually incomprehensible and means little to most of us. Context makes the problem space that we are entering more compelling. The 2006 "digital universe" is estimated to be more than three million times the information contained in all the books produced in the history of the world. By 2010, the study forecasts that this "digital universe" will increase in production by more than six fold to a staggering 988 exabytes per year.

In other words, the vast majority of our intellectual information is now being produced, not in print, but in digital formats. Further complicating matters, we are producing more than we ever have produced before. How will we ever sift through, access, transport, secure, and preserve the important bits of our cultural record?

Enter digital libraries.

Wikipedia and various other sources define "digital library" as a "library in which collections are stored in digital formats (as opposed to print, microform, or other media) and accessible by computers."[1] Delving into this definition, we note that the library is an organized body that holds collections – digital objects that have been grouped into categories, presumably for access purposes.

So the cultural record now depends upon *digital* library collections that increasingly bring structure to the digital deluge, and that allow us to make this content useful to its worldwide audiences. These digital libraries, unlike their physical counterparts, are a relatively new phenomenon. Physical libraries with organizational schemes have arguably existed since at least 300 BCE when

Aristotle helped to create the Great Library of Alexandria. Physical libraries have long-established methods of collecting, organizing, and preserving information. Likewise, they have a long history of continued existence.

Digital libraries, on the other hand, are still in their infancy. The field of digital libraries is still emerging and does not yet have firmly established practices in place. The good news is that, as with most field formations, there is much experimentation, research, and production activity happening throughout the world as the field begins to define its parameters. The more troubling news is that much of this experimentation will, in all likelihood, ultimately fail. This situation demands that we both record and share our early strides as digital libraries and that we begin to answer a series of questions regarding the sustainability of the digital structures that our culture is creating.

SUSTAINABILITY

How can we hope to sustain these digital resources that we are creating apace? How will we transport, store, secure, and replicate all of this information? And when those resources are part of a digital library – broadly defined – how can we sustain the range of library apparati that undergird these resources?

Merely broaching this topic raises several important questions:

- How do we build sustainability into these new operations, not only in terms of funding streams but the entire complex of stabilizing processes and institutional forms that lend sustainability to resources? What is needed, structurally, to sustain digital libraries once they are created?

- If we don't have effective structures to sustain digital libraries yet (and this seems likely), how do we create them? Institutionalization takes time to permeate society in terms of accepted practice. Will we have the requisite time, or will we see an intervening digital dark age when the majority of the knowledge created by society is lost?

- Given the proliferating pace of information cited above, how can we know (or guess?) what to sustain? The only certainty we can really claim to know is that we will not be able to preserve everything, but must apply some degree of prioritization to the task at hand.

- Theorists ranging from Huseyin Leblebici and Timothy Dowd to Clayton Christensen have demonstrated that successful innovations most often happen on the periphery, not at the center, of a market.[2] How can we anticipate which of the many flowers now blooming may be the crucial ones to devote scarce resources to sustaining (or at least preserving)? And how patient must we remain in order to allow this drama to unfold at its own pace?

The contributors to this volume have some tentative advice to offer by way of inter-institutional collaboration, or at least coordination. In some cases they have put forward new cooperative organizational models to share the burden of supporting new operations. There are many opportunities for aligning institutional practices to take advantages of scale and unified workflows.

For every 50 experiments, we may have to realistically expect 49 to perish. We need to watch for the innovations on the fringes that demonstrate unexpected vitality, and accept the fact that unsuccessful attempts will pass away.

THE ESSAYS

Our contributors explore the topic of sustaining digital libraries from many different perspectives:

Paul Berkman distinguishes between digital and other mediums that preceded it. He highlights unique aspects of the medium and the elements that are necessary to sustain a digital object. Berkman looks at both the tasks of sustaining digital objects and sustaining organizations that are responsible stewards of those objects. He engages with the necessary economic and political strategies, and concludes that digital information sustainability is key to the knowledge management and discovery opportunities that will empower an enlightened society into the future

Tyler Walters highlights the need for strategic partnerships, arguing that interdependence is a necessary element in sustaining scholarly digital resources. He proposes a sustainability model comprised of four elements: Organization, technology, economic, and collection-based sustainability. Walters uses the MetaArchive Cooperative, an inter-institutional preservation organization, and its host organization, the Educopia Institute, as a case study to explore how employing this model of interdependence enables important community-based initiatives to become stable over the long term

Bradley Daigle explores the impact of the digital medium on scholarly enterprises and the academic publishing market. He points to the problems inherent in employing old strategies and methodologies when engaging in a new medium. Daigle analyzes the relationship between new scholarship forms and the new library environments needed to support those new forms. Like Walters, Daigle proposes that strategic partnerships pose the best opportunity for libraries to lead the way in this emergent arena and to continue to serve as support for the apparatus of humanities scholarship. Finally, Daigle looks at the need for both infrastructure development and the creation of economic models for such stewardship of cultural assets in digital form, using the University of Virginia as a case study.

Michael Furlough examines the recent activities of libraries as production centers for digital scholarship and the corresponding shift that must take place in the library's mission in order to organizationally sustain these activities. He uses Penn State University's press and library to illustrate changing relationships between these entities due to the emergence of digital scholarship.

Leslie Johnston uses Fedora and the University of Virginia's digital collections repository to outline a model for employing digital curation principles and practices to sustain digital repositories. She keeps a primary aim in sight: long-term usability of collections and objects. Johnston pays attention not only to the curation activities and technical infrastructure, but also to the *social* infrastructure – the degree to which a repository and its sustainability is integrated into the overall institutional mission.

Mary Marlino, Tamara Sumner, Karon Kelly, and Michael Wright share the strategies that they have developed and undertaken to provide a sustainability plan for the Digital Library for Earth System Education (DLESE). Their detailed analysis of costs and specific planning tasks provides a practical case study of what is required for sustainability efforts.

CONCLUSIONS

> One of the greatest discoveries a man makes, one of his great surprises, is to find he can do what he was afraid he couldn't do.
>
> - Henry Ford

We conclude with a few summary observations of our own as both editors of this book and leaders within the emerging field of digital libraries. These observations are offered as words of encouragement to our many colleagues searching for models to carry forward their compelling accomplishments in digital libraries. While the task of sustaining these efforts may frequently seem like an impossible task, we believe that there are many signs of hope for our field. When asked, "Can we sustain digital libraries?" we will answer forthrightly: **Yes, we can.**

Incremental Sustainability

Our first observation is that sustainability claims only make sense in some relatively constrained time frame. Nothing is sustainable forever. Given the shifting sands upon which we currently stand, we should not ask *"Is this digital library sustainable?"* but rather *"How long can we be confident of sustaining this digital library at this moment?"* The answer to the first question is always an ambiguous question mark. The answer to the second question can be honest, realistic, and backed up with concrete evidence.

A further corollary is that the incremental progress we make toward sustaining any given digital library will provide us with growing evidence on which to base subsequent claims and initiatives. Such progress will also hopefully grant us a growing base of support from users of digital libraries, whether that support is commercial or institutional.

This observation should be seen as common sense, applicable to almost any kind of program, whether a digital library or other kind of service operation. Businesses look at financial forecasts constantly, and increasingly traditional print libraries do as well. The assumption of indefinite sustainability of all traditional library operations has been demonstrated to be false as more and more "givens" in traditional libraries go by the wayside. The question is really (*and always should have been*) what slate of information service offerings is desirable enough that stakeholders will sustain it? This issue brings us to our next observation.

Digital Libraries May Be *More* Sustainable

Because of the utility of the functions that digital libraries provide, it may be that they are *more* sustainable, not less, than traditional libraries – perhaps *much* more sustainable. Again taking a broad perspective on what constitutes a digital library operation, one does not have to go beyond the colossus of Google to find a service that is ubiquitously used by academics (along with everyone else). This company is a powerhouse economically and technically, and shows every sign of being as sustainable as any digital library reasonably can be today.

Does this mean that we can already claim victory for digital libraries and believe that they will have the longevity of print archives? No. We may legitimately be skeptical of the long term sustainability of even a behemoth like Google if our timescale is hundreds of years. But this comes back to the point about incremental claims of sustainability. We simply do not have enough accumulated history of digital libraries to make any claims credibly in a timescale of centuries. We *can* observe, at least in theory, that bits can be replicated indefinitely, whereas physical media degrade with time. On theoretical grounds, digital libraries may again be more sustainable than traditional libraries.

Critiques of Google and other Internet search engines by research librarians often miss (or ignore) the point that these businesses provide a critically useful information service to academic stakeholders. Indeed, the link analysis algorithms used by Google could be seen as comparable to (though certainly not the same as) some of the features of peer review. Sustainability follows value and utility in our view, and the sooner we internalize this point the sooner our digital library services will become sustainable. This observation brings us to our last point.

If You Build Something They Want, They Will Come and Sustain It

Ultimately there may not be any great mystery about how to sustain digital libraries. Simply put, create something that researchers will insist that you continue to provide and that will inspire them to lend their support toward making it an institutional funding priority. If the resource or service cannot pass this simple litmus test, then it probably is not worth sustaining anyway.

Research communities evolve over time and it may or may not be the case that the perceived permanence of programs like traditional libraries and archives will be replicated in the digital library sphere. The possibility that such information services may have shorter tenure than ossified services based on benign neglect of print resources does not mean that digital libraries are less valuable or useful for researchers, it may mean that they may have more rapid cycles of evolution.

Is this a bad thing? We do not think so. Quite the contrary, the fact that digital library services evolve quickly is a great strength and source of vitality. The service that adapts quickly to take advantage of new opportunities may also adapt quickly to new opportunities for sustainability. The complaint is often heard that digital library services rely on "soft funding" that "cannot be counted on." But if a service cannot attract both opportunistic soft funding and a level of ongoing support, then it probably does not represent a fundamentally viable value proposition for researchers.

We are poised at the beginning of a new era in which we may bring forward the most successful elements of past practices and combine them with the innovations made possible by changes in technology, despite the challenges they have posed to the status quo for librarianship. The coming years will continue to be exhilarating ones for the pioneers of this new field, who we celebrate as explorers of new intellectual spaces, and who write the future in their tentative steps across this unsettled shore.

NOTES

1. Wikipedia, http://en.wikipedia.org/wiki/Digital_library (accessed on January 24, 2008).
2. See Huseyin Leblebici, Gerald R. Salancik, Anne Copay, and Tom King. "Institutional Change and the Transformation of Interorganizational Fields: An Organizational History of the U.S. Broadcasting Industry." *Administrative Science Quarterly* 36 (1991): 333-363; Timothy Dowd "Musical Diversity and the Mainstream Recording Market, 1950 to 1990." *Rassegna Italiana di Sociologia* 41 (2000): 223-263 and "Structural Power and the Construction of Markets: The Case of Rhythm and Blues." *Comparative Social Research* 21 (2003): 147-201; and Clayton Christensen. 1997. *The Innovator's Dilemma: When New Technologies Cause Great Firms to Fail* (Boston, MA: Harvard Business School Press).

REFERENCES CITED

Gantz, John F., David Reinsel, Christopher Chcute, Wolfgang Schlichting, John McArthur, Stephen Minton, Irita Xheneti, Anna Toncheva, and Alex Manfrediz. 2007. "The Expanding Digital Universe: A Forecast of Worldwide Information Growth Through 2010." IDC and EMC White Paper, available at http://www.emc.com/collateral/analyst-reports/expanding-digital-idc-white-paper.pdf (accessed on December 14, 2007).

ONCE IN A HUNDRED GENERATIONS

Paul Arthur Berkman (University of California, Santa Barbara)

Abstract: Once in a hundred generations – every 2,000 years – an information technology threshold is reached that changes human capacity to manage and discover knowledge. Invention of the digital medium created such a paradigm shift and we are now faced with the challenge of sustaining the information products generated with this transformational technology. For the last several thousand years, libraries and archives have provided the architectures to manage information based on their content and context, respectively. With digital technologies, however, the inherent structure of information (i.e., boundaries between granules of content) also can be applied to information management. Lessons learned from the National Science Digital Library (http://www.nsdl.org) reveal that technological as well as organizational and economic strategies are necessary to sustain digital libraries as "public goods." Implementation of a national task force on digital library sustainability is recommended to elaborate visionary solutions for knowledge management and discovery in our evolving digital era.

A BRIEF HISTORY OF HUMAN COMMUNICATION

Understanding where we have been is a key to the future. The opportunity to transform human communication on a global scale happens once in a hundred generations – every 2,000 years – and we are living during such a period (Fig. 1.1).

Question 1: What are the distinctions between the digital medium and all of its hardcopy predecessors?

For thousands of years Neolithic humans shared their life stories on cave walls (with smoke handprints and colored animal drawings) or on rocks (with stick figures and symbols) etched for future generations. Immovable, these images on stone have weathered the test of time.

Then, nearly 5,500 years ago, clay tablets awakened a new capacity for humans to share experiences and insights. Rolling devices – the ancestor of all typesetting – enabled humans to imprint and reproduce symbols in clay. Clay also had the advantage of being much easier to transport than stone, but it was more fragile.

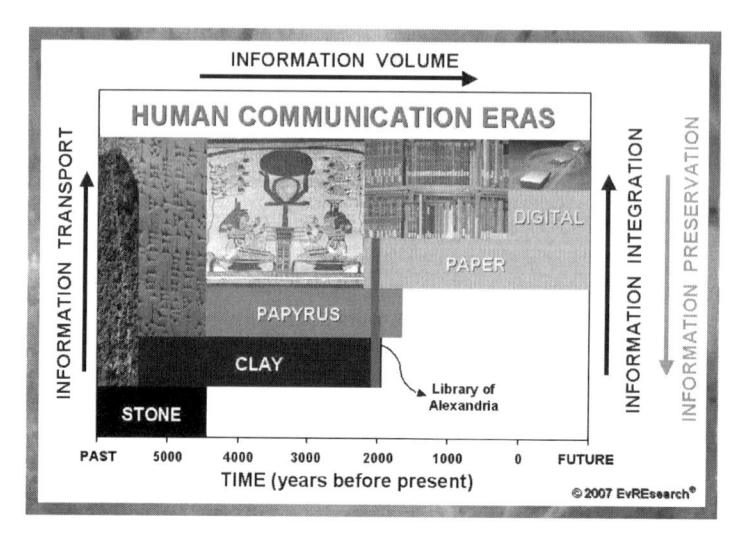

FIGURE 1.1: Eras in our civilization based on the media that humans have used to communicate beyond face-to-face. Each new communication medium has increased human capacity to: (a) transport information across time and space; (b) produce more information faster; and (c) integrate information into relational schema. Conversely, information has become more ethereal and difficult to preserve from stone to digital. Modified from Berkman et al. (2006a,b).

A thousand years later, humans invented papyrus to exchange information with much greater detail and color than ever before. Papyrus was lighter and more pliable than clay, which made it easier to distribute. Pieces of papyrus also could be combined to create complex information sources.

After another two millennia, we saw the advent of paper, which certainly must rank as one of the most significant inventions in our civilization. During this period with the Great Library of Alexandria, clay, papyrus, and paper coexisted as media to share data and other information beyond face-to-face communication. On a global scale, paper then took off as the principal medium for communicating across space and time.

Until the invention (or rather harnessing) of electricity, paper was unrivaled in the role of sharing knowledge in our world. Then came digital devices to collect, store, transmit, and display information. It has only been in the past fifty years that digital devices have become the communication backbone in our world information society.

Each era of global communication, from stone to digital (Fig. 1.1), has been accompanied by a threshold increase in human capacity to transport information. Similarly, each new communication medium has significantly increased our capacity to produce information, as indicated by the relative volumes of information that emerged. Moreover, the ability to integrate information has increased over time with tablets, folios, books, and now websites.

In contrast, the most resilient medium was stone with petroglyphs and pictographs that have stood the test of time through rain, snow, wind, and even fire. Subsequent media have been much more fragile. In fact, the digital medium has been like a black hole where most of the information produced has been lost because of limited preservation strategies and rapid obsolescence of storage devices.

Over the past 6,000 years, there has been global transformation in the information management medium every couple millennia. Paper was most recent with its invention in China around 2,000 years ago, curiously near the start of the Common Era that has since marked time across our civilization. If the past is any indication of the future, the digital medium will be with us for millennia to come. The challenge is to manage our digital information and to facilitate knowledge discovery for the benefit of future generations around the world.

KNOWLEDGE MANAGEMENT AND DISCOVERY

Looking backward through time, we recognize that information in our civilization has been managed largely through libraries and archives. While similar in their needs to facilitate information access and preservation, these two architectures possess fundamental differences. Archives manage information based on the *context* of records linked to specific activities and transactions, like the Bureau of Motor Vehicle records of your car title. Libraries largely manage information based on the *content* of the information resources, as with the subject categories in the Dewey Decimal System. Beyond content and context there is a third element of information to establish meaning and that is its *structure* (Fig. 1.2).

Question 2: Are there unique aspects of the digital medium that will enhance knowledge management and discovery?

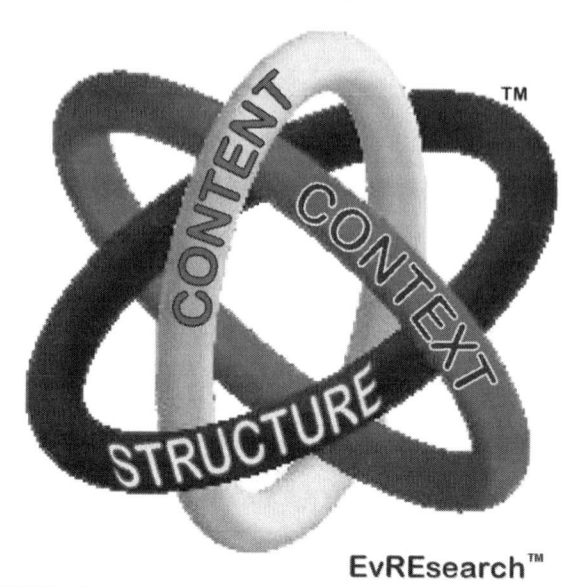

FIGURE 1.2: "Borromean Rings of Meaning" illustrate the three inseparable elements of information (content, context, and structure) that provide the basis for understanding and synthesizing knowledge. From Berkman et al. (2006a,b).

For example, when a message is encrypted (i.e., the *structure* is altered) it still has *content* and *context*, but no meaning absent the key to unlock the encryption. Alternatively, if the names or dates and places are removed from an information resource, it still has *context* and *structure*, but limited meaning without the salient facts. Similarly, meaning will be compromised by removing the context that can be used to authenticate an information resource or establish its provenance.

The paradigm shift created by digital technologies is the opportunity to dynamically utilize the *structure* of information as well as its *content* and *context* for the purposes of knowledge management and discovery. A hardcopy book can be managed based on its *content* (as in libraries) or its *context* (as in archives). However, it is not possible to automatically break a printed book into smaller granules of information (chapters, pages, paragraphs, etc.) that can be managed or discovered independently.

With the digital medium it has become possible to utilize the *content* and *context* as well as *structural* patterns (such as the white space formed by an indent or carriage return) to manage sets, subsets, and supersets of information resources. It is this ability to dynamically manage the granularity of information that distinguishes the digital medium from all of its hardcopy predecessors in our civilization (Fig. 1.1).

Content, context, and *structure* of information create meaning that can be interpreted across a spectrum of understanding (Liebowitz 1999). The value of information is that it provides the foundation to synthesize knowledge that enables individuals to determine the course of their actions. Knowledge, which can be simply defined in terms of information relationships, is the epitome of learning (Bloom 1956) and the aspiration of all educated people.

DIGITAL INFORMATION SUSTAINABILITY

Digital libraries and archives, which are emerging around the world (Arms 2000; Thibodeau 2001; NDIIPP 2002; Greenstein and Thorin 2002; Hodges et al. 2003; Lesk 2004; Duranti 2005), reflect the issues of sustainability. The following lessons are from the *National Science, Technology, Engineering and Mathematics Education Digital Library*, or NSDL, (http://www.nsdl.org) that originated in 2000 as a "community based endeavor" supported by the National Science Foundation (http://www.nsf.gov).

The NSDL established a "working structure" with a *Core-Integration Team*, *Policy Committee*, five *Standing Committees*, a *National Visiting Committee* and other entities as approved by an *Assembly* of the projects (http://sustain.comm.nsdl.org/). Supported projects contribute to the NSDL program by producing collections and services that have value to user, producer, and sponsor communities. Technical innovations are woven throughout so that the digital library can be effectively operated and applied. Generalizing, the NSDL "working structure" reveals underlying sustainability elements of any digital information organization (Table 1.1).

TABLE 1.1: Sustainability Elements of Digital Information Organizations[a]

ELEMENT	SCOPE OF ACTIVITIES
Program	Long-term administrative strategies for collaboration among developers, users, sponsors, and other stakeholders to "anchor" the digital information organization
Projects	Public-private-university-government strategies to support the creation, maintenance, funding and evolution of needed collections and services
Communities	Engagement, networking, and evaluation strategies to meet the demands of users, developers, and sponsors
Technical	Application strategies to achieve long-term preservation, access, and knowledge discovery with digital information

[a] See the Sustainability Standing Committee homepage (http://sustain.comm.nsdl.org/). Adapted from Berkman (2004).

Organizational strategies to implement the NSDL are further reflected by the projects that have been funded, effectively in two phases before and after 2003 (Fig. 1.3). Between 2000 and 2003, NSDL funded 88 collection, 45 service, 29 *Core Integration*, and 19 research projects. In 2004, characteristics of the NSDL conceptually changed with elimination of the track for collection projects and the emergence of pathways projects "to provide stewardship for the content and services needed by major communities of learners" (http://www.nsdl.org). From 2004 to 2006, there have been an additional 31 *Core Integration*, 21 pathways, 22 service, and eight research project awards. Together, these NSDL awards have been distributed across 35 states (NSDL 2007).

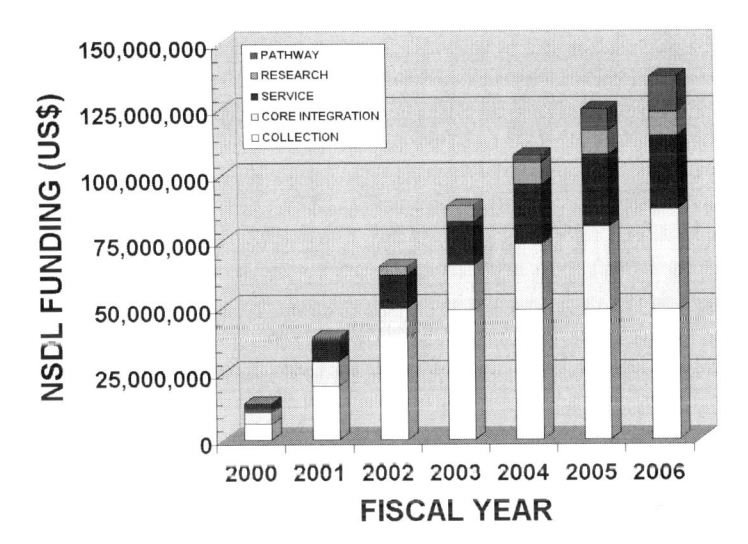

FIGURE 1.3: Cumulative funding by the National Science Foundation for different types of projects (legend) in the National Science, Technology, Engineering, and Mathematics Education Digital Library (http://www.nsdl.org). Data are from NSDL (2007).

In addition to conceptual changes, the shift in organizational emphasis before and after 2003 is represented by the relative support for *Core Integration*, which is responsible for integrating the NSDL projects. During the 2000-2003 period, *Core Integration* accounted for 16% of the projects and 19% of the NSDL funding. Afterward, these percentages increased to 34% and 43%, respectively. These adjustments in the NSDL reflect the distributed-centralized continuum of architectures that can be implemented for digital information organizations in general.

Question 3: What is the optimal allocation of resources to balance the elements (Table 1.1) that are needed to sustain a digital information organization?

FUNDING PUBLIC GOODS

To better understand the economics of digital libraries, stories from NSDL projects that were considered to be sustainable were captured in a series of written vignettes (Table 1.2). These projects all existed prior to 2000 and provide potential anchors for long-term development of the NSDL organization, which is why many of them have received pathways funding.

TABLE 1.2: Matrix of "Sustainability Vignettes" Written for the NSDL[b]

NSDL PROJECT	USERS	FUNDING	STRUCTURE
Earth Science Information Partnership Federation: http://esipfed.org Formed 1998	370 on list server; 83 partners include national data centers	government, meeting registration	not-for-profit corporation (federated partnership)
Electronic Environmental Resources Library: http://eerl.org Formed 1994	Educators, librarians (about 3,000 visitors/day)	government, university gifts, corporations	not-for-profit corporation
Journal of Chemical Education: http://jce.divched.org JCE founded 1924. NSDL pathways funding 2006	Chemical science teachers (about 12,000)	government, corporation, subscription, advertising	not-for-profit corporation (division within professional society)
The Macaulay Library: http://birds.cornell.edu/macaulaylibrary/ Audio collection initiated 1930s with Cornell Laboratory of Ornithology	museums, science centers, educators, researchers, corporations	government, university, gifts, sales	not-for-profit corporation (membership organization within university)
Mathematical Association of America Digital Library: http://mathdl.ma.org & **Math Gateway:** http://mathgateway.maa.org MAA incorporated 1920. NSDL pathways funding 2004	about 15,000 visitors daily	government	not-for-profit corporation
WGBH – Teachers' Domain: http://teachersdomain.org WGBH radio began 1951. NSDL pathways funding 2004.	K-12 teachers and students (about 60,000 registered)	government, corporations, gifts, licensing	not-for-profit corporation (department within local media network)

[b]See the Sustainability Standing Committee homepage — http://sustain.comm.nsdl.org/

All of the vignette projects involve not-for-profit corporations, suggesting that a corporate framework is necessary for large or small digital information organizations to manage their fiscal and legal responsibilities in a sustainable manner. Moreover, all of the vignette projects involve government funding to produce results that can be openly disseminated, which effectively makes them *"public goods"* (Varian 1998, Stiglitz 1999). As such, these projects produce non-rival resources that can be consumed by anyone without diminishing the availability for others.

A significant hurdle for the NSDL, as with many digital information organizations, is to leverage current support into future revenue streams that will promote its long-term stability. Government agencies, universities, and other institutions with public mandates, resilient infrastructures, and access to long-term support may provide societal anchors to sustain networks of digital information resources. Philanthropic contributions, as with the Carnegie libraries (Bobinski 1969, Slyck 1995), also may be part of the solution. Moreover, sustainability likely will involve strategies to sell valued information goods and services (Stein 2007), such as providing access to scholarly journals through online databases (http://www.jstor.org/).

Question 4: How is value established with digital information organizations that user, sponsor, and developer communities (Table 1.1) will financially support?

CONCLUSION

From stone to digital (Fig. 1.1), each era of global communication has been accompanied by a threshold increase in human capacity to transport, produce, and integrate information. As a civilization, our legacy is wrapped into this information that historically has been safeguarded in libraries and archives.

However, we have yet to build the information management architectures that will effectively preserve digital information (Boeke 2006). Technical difficulties with long-term preservation underscore the challenges to sustain digital information over decades, let alone centuries and millennia. The above types of questions underlie the technical, organizational, and economic issues that must be considered to sustain digital information organizations.

Practical strategies to sustain digital information in the public good will come from targeted discussions that engage stakeholder experts throughout society to think out-of-the-box into the distant future. Along these lines, in January 2005, a national task force on digital library sustainability was proposed to twelve federal agencies through the *Federal Science and Technology Information Managers Group* (http://www.cendi.gov/minutes/pa_0105.html). The closing panel of the NSDL annual meeting in October 2006 and a subsequent discussion at the Library of Congress (http://www.digitalpreservation.gov/) in November 2006 further revealed actionable interest in implementing such a task force (minutes of meetings can be accessed through the NSDL Sustainability Standing Committee homepage: http://sustain.comm.nsdl.org).

We are living during a rare transition between global communication eras – which happens once in a hundred generations (Fig. 1.1) – and there is no roadmap. It is clear, however, that digital information sustainability is essential to the knowledge management and discovery opportunities that will empower an enlightened society.

Our generation has serious responsibilities to manage digital information into the future for, as observed by the convener of the *United Nations World Summit on the Information Society* (http://www.itu.int/wsis/), Adama Samassekou (personal communication 2004):

"Knowledge is the common wealth of humanity."

ACKNOWLEDGEMENTS

I thank the diverse members of the Sustainability Standing Committee (SSC) for sharing insights, passion and creativity to sustain the *National Science, Technology, Engineering and Mathematics Education Digital Library* (NSDL). The opportunity to craft this paper, as chair of the SSC, was generously supported by the NSDL (Grant No. NSF / DUE 0329044).

REFERENCES

Arms, William Y. 2000. *Digital libraries.* Cambridge: MIT Press.

Berkman, Paul A. 2004. Sustaining the National Science Digital Library. *Project Kaleidoscope Newsletter.* August 20, 2004 http://www.pkal.org/template2.cfm?c_id=1383.

Berkman, Paul A., George J. Morgan, Reagan Moore, Babak Hamidzadeh. 2006a. Automated granularity to integrate digital records: The "Antarctic treaty searchable database" case study. *Data Science Journal* 5:84-99. http://www.jstage.jst.go.jp/article/dsj/5/0/84/_pdf.

--. 2006b. Automated granularity to integrate digital records: The "Antarctic treaty searchable database" case study. *Data Science*

Journal 5:84-99. Translation – Archivo Municipal, Cartagena, Spain. http://archivo.cartagena.es/recursos/texto0_antarctica_dos.pdf.

Bobinski, George. 1969. *Carnegie Libraries: Their History and Impact on American Public Library Development*. Chicago: American Library Association.

Boeke, Cindy. 2006. IPRES 2006 conference report: Digital preservation takes off in the e-environment. *D-Lib Magazine* 12, no. 12. http://www.dlib.org/dlib/december06/boeke/12boeke.html.

Bloom Benjamin S. 1956. *Taxonomy of educational objectives, handbook I: The cognitive domain*. New York: David McKay.

Duranti. Luciana (ed.). 2005. *The long-term preservation of authentic electronic records: Findings of the InterPARES Project*. San Miniato: Archilab. http://www.interpares.org/book/index.htm.

Greenstein, David I. and Thorin, Suzanne E. 2002. *The Digital Library: A Biography*. 2nd Edition. Washington, D.C.: Digital Library Federation.

Hodges, Patricia, Maria Bonn, Mark Sandler, and John P. Wilkin, (eds.). 2003. *Digital libraries: A vision for the 21st century*. Ann Arbor: University of Michigan Scholarly Publishing Office.

Lesk, Michael. 2004. *Understanding digital libraries*. 2nd Edition. New York: Morgan Kaufmann.

Liebowitz, Jay (ed.). 1999. *Knowledge management handbook*. Boca Raton: CRC Press.

NSDL. 2007. *2006 annual report: Leveraging collaborative networks*. Boulder: National Science Digital Library. http://nsdl.org/about/download/misc/NSDL_ANNUAL_REPORT_2006.pdf.

NDIIPP. 2002. *Preserving our digital heritage: Plan for the national digital information infrastructure and preservation program* Washington, D.C.: Library of Congress.

Stein, Seth. 2007. Education, Outreach and Marketing. *EOS Transactions of the American Geophysical Union*. 88, no. 4:39-40. http://www.agu.org/pubs/crossref/2007/2007EO040007.shtml.

Stiglitz, Joseph E. 1999. Knowledge as a public good. In *Global public goods*, eds. Kaul, Inge, Isabelle Grunberg, and Marc Stern, 308-326. Oxford. Oxford Scholarship Online Monographs.

Slyck, Abigail A.V. 1995. *Free to all: Carnegie libraries and American culture, 1890-1920*. Chicago: University of Chicago Press.

Thibodeau, Kenneth. 2001. Building the archives of the future: Advances in preserving electronic records at the National Archives and Records Administration. *D-Lib Magazine* 7, no. 2. http://www.dlib.org/dlib/february01/thibodeau/02thibodeau.html.

Varian, Hal R. 1998. *Markets for information goods*. Berkeley: University of California.

Digital Sustainability: Weaving a Tapestry of Interdependency to Advance Digital Library Programs

Tyler O. Walters (Georgia Institute of Technology)

Abstract: Today's digital libraries are growing in their technological interconnectivity. However, to build and sustain scholarly digital resources, the funders and parent institutions of digital libraries also must become increasingly interdependent. This essay examines digital library sustainability from the perspective of social and knowledge networks. A generalizable model is presented to introduce four major modes of sustainability – organization, technology, economic, and collections. To illustrate how a digital library organization can address these four modes, the model is applied to the MetaArchive Cooperative, a multi-university digital preservation partnership founded through the Library of Congress' National Digital Information Infrastructure and Preservation Program (NDIIPP). As the model is applied to and guides the Cooperative's activities, it produces a strong social network of partnering organizations. This socio-organizational network provides the infrastructure and sources of support required to sustain the MetaArchive Cooperative's activities and achieve its digital preservation goals. The need to build such relationships between institutions, consortia, organizations, high-level strategic partners, and other entities is greater than ever before. Weaving this tapestry of interdependency is the next step individual organizations need to take to improve digital library sustainability.

INTRODUCTION

With the advent of the World Wide Web and the release of the first free browser, Mosaic, in 1993, the popular revolution in digital information began. A decade-and-a-half later, digital collections abound and their managers increasingly ask themselves how they are going to sustain their digital activity. Sustaining digital libraries over great periods of time is a defining challenge of our day. As Paul A. Berkman writes, "Once in a hundred generations – every 2,000 years – an information technology threshold is reached that changes human capacity to manage and discover knowledge. Invention of the digital medium created such a paradigm shift and we are now faced with the challenge of sustaining the information products generated with this transformational technology."[1] Libraries and archives have been managing paper-based information objects for the last couple thousand years – how do we now do this in the digital paradigm? While there is no simple solution to sustaining digital libraries, perhaps the best approach is to develop collections using the concepts of social and knowledge network theory.

Such an approach requires multiple layers of effort. Gone are the days when a library built its own systems with no regard for how other libraries would use them. Today, there are application technologies to develop jointly and share, content formats to maintain and standardize, collections to preserve through common best practices, digital library programs to sustain collectively, and much more. To make all of this work, organizations must develop content standards and interoperable technologies, such as the Open Archives Initiative Protocol for Metadata Harvesting (OAI-PMH). Technologies like the OAI Protocol require organizational collaboration and integration, and they result in interconnections at many levels. As William Arms recently wrote, "No digital library is an island. The question is how to make the islands fit together as an archipelago."[2] Much like the growing level of technological interconnectivity, the organizations, programs, and funding models involved in creating our cyberinfrastructure must become increasingly interdependent to sustain today's digital resources as well as build the invaluable digital collections of tomorrow.

This essay utilizes social and knowledge network theory in order to build a longitudinal model for sustainability that focuses on collaboration, integration, interconnection, and organizational networking to sustain innovation in digital library development.[3] Four major modes of sustainability are introduced – organization, technology, economic, and collections. To illustrate how a digital library organization might address these four modes of sustainability, the model is applied to the MetaArchive Cooperative, a multi-university digital preservation partnership with the Library of Congress' National Digital Information Infrastructure and Preservation Program (NDIIPP).

THE BUILDING BLOCKS – MODES OF SUSTAINABILITY FOR DIGITAL LIBRARIES

Sustaining the products of human organization and communication requires a multi-faceted body of activities. Similarly, there are many facets to the concept of digital library sustainability. First, people come together and organize themselves in units of work (e.g. libraries) to create tangible information goods and services. To continue their activities, these library organizations must be sustained as they change to meet societal needs. This issue is addressed as the concept of *organization sustainability*. The technologies these organizations use to create their goods and services will evolve, but they also need to be sustained so the organization can continue its activities. This issue is known as *technology sustainability*. Organizations require financial resources to employ people and technologies to produce their goods and services. They must also collect enough finances to at least meet their expenses. This concept is called *economic sustainability*. Lastly, in the world of digital libraries, collections of digital information are created and managed. Sustaining these information products over time is called *collections sustainability*. Let us now delve into each of these "modes" of sustainability more deeply.

One important building block toward achieving program goals in digital libraries is to sustain the organizations that create and support the programs. **Organization sustainability** refers to strategies that advance collaborations between organizational units or subunits to increase a program's functions and/or to achieve a particular goal. These strategies can be applied within one parent institution (e.g., a library, IT, distance learning, and an academic department working together within a university) or between parent institutions (e.g., units of several universities working together). The collaborating units or institutions undertake a planned and coordinated group of activities to achieve a specific purpose (e.g., the preservation of digital library content, as is the case with the program of the MetaArchive Cooperative).[4] The following is a hypothetical model in which organization sustainability is achieved by constructing layers of interconnections between organizations.

First, a single institution, with its resources and expertise, presents a goal or goals to similar institutions. Second, if enough interest is generated, a consortium is formed to create a program for accomplishing the goal(s). The consortium generates additional value and elements of sustainability that the individual institutions cannot generate on their own. In other words, the sum of the whole (i.e., the program) is greater than its parts (i.e., the institutions). At this level, long-term collaboration between projects, users, sponsors, agencies, and other stakeholders is present. Third, a nonprofit management entity to host the consortium is formed. This nonprofit provides further strategic guidance and support for organizational sustainability and program development. This entity facilitates relationships with other organizations and consortia and provides a low-cost, low-overhead conduit from which to gather and manage fiscal resources. Fourth, the consortium links itself to larger national and international digital library development agendas. This last step fosters proper strategic alignment, funding, and additional access to expertise and new knowledge. These collaborative networks are formed because the challenge of digital preservation is bigger than any single institution. "Collaborating with other organizations is necessary," as H. Brinton Milward and Keith G. Provan write, "if there is any hope of making progress in effectively managing the problem."[5] Thus, the original consortium interweaves itself with many other institutions, consortia, private organizations, government agencies, and expansive strategies to provide access to a wealth of resources, financial and otherwise, while also connecting people with a diversity of knowledge, skills, and interests.

Technology sustainability refers to strategies that advance collaborative creation, dissemination, and maintenance of technologies. Libraries are investing much energy into open source software applications like DSpace, Fedora, LOCKSS, and Sakai; harvesting utilities like OAI-PMH; and middleware like Shibboleth. By supporting and contributing to the open source model, libraries hope to achieve long-term sustainability concerning the technological structure of their collections.[6] Similar to the organization sustainability mode of the model, the technology mode relies upon building layers of interconnections.

First, an initial group of development partners gives birth to new technology or software. It is nurtured and brought to market with its source code visible, where early adopters utilize it. Second, the number of development partners grows as new developers from these early adopting institutions contribute their expertise and resources to further the technology's development. The technology begins to stabilize and mature, gaining a critical mass of users. Adopting groups of developers and users form. Third, following today's trend, a governing and coordinating organization is created around the developer and user groups, much like the nonprofit management entity hosting the consortium in the organization sustainability mode. Examples are the DSpace Consortium Inc., LOCKSS Alliance, Fedora Project, Sakai Foundation, the Internet2 Consortium's management of

Shibboleth, and the Open Archives Initiative's management of its protocol for metadata harvesting.[7] Many of these follow the approach for establishing open source governing organizations set by the Apache Software Foundation. These technology development organizations create a mixed base of funding from their host institutions, foundations, government agencies, and corporate entities. These organizations then serve as conduits for innovation and expertise, and they provide financial and infrastructural resources to develop new technologies addressing the needs of digital libraries, academic research, and university-based learning. These and other technology development organizations bear studying as they evolve and attempt to sustain their technologies.

Economic sustainability refers to the revenues and investments necessary to support digital libraries. As with the earlier modes of sustainability – organizational and technological – the economic mode also matures through the successful construction of layers of interdependency. At each level mentioned thus far, there are resource inputs of finances, infrastructure, and expertise, all with monetary value. Individual institutions and the initial development partner group provide a base of economic inputs. In a consortium, and in the adopting developer and user groups, these inputs combine to generate new ideas and new infrastructures. These groups also seek funding and apply it to their existing economic resources. The nonprofit management entity and governing organizations bring more partners, projects, and consortia together in pursuit of generating funds (and new knowledge) to carry out their objectives. Lastly, aligning these entities with national and international strategic partnerships helps to identify further revenues to infuse the projects.

In addition to all of these layers, goods and services are provided directly to interested consumers to generate additional revenue. These revenues are not intended to meet all costs incurred by the technology developing organization but rather to provide one of several necessary revenue streams. All of these sources of funding, from partnerships and other associations to fees for goods and services, must combine to meet the financial expenses and investment needs that organizations incur while developing and sustaining their digital libraries.

After outlining the first three aspects of sustainability – organization, technology, and economic – a question remains. Are there other significant aspects of sustainability to consider? There is at least one – the sustainability of digital collections themselves. **Collections sustainability** refers to strategies for ensuring that the inherent qualities of information resources persist. These qualities must be maintained for the resources to be valuable to their producers and end users. Cultural and information resources have at least three major, inherent characteristics: (1) the context of their creation and maintenance, (2) the content they hold, and (3) their structures as objects. While the concept of "collections sustainability" relates closely to technology sustainability, it is not the same.

The term *provenance* refers to this first issue of "context of creation," addressing the social and organizational processes that create and maintain the information, data, or records in question. Understanding the "context" or provenance of digital objects is critical to their long-term usability and significance. For instance, the data management field recognizes the need to document context by applying the concept known as *data provenance*. Data provenance refers to the "process of tracing and recording the origins of data and its movement between databases. Provenance is now an acute issue in scientific databases where it's central to the validation of data."[8] Scholars and researchers using data, as well as data managers, realize it is critically important to know where certain pieces of data in a database originated when attempting to determine the genuineness of the data and the veracity of research findings. Therefore, we must sustain at least two inherent qualities of information – authenticity and reliability. Information is authentic when it has not been "changed or manipulated after it has been created or received or migrated over the whole continuum of information creation, maintenance, and preservation."[9] So, *authenticity* focuses on the need for the unchanging nature of information, its content, context, and structure.[10] *Reliability* differs from authenticity in that it refers to the quality or truthfulness of the information content, as opposed to whether or not the informational content has changed or unchanged. Specifically, reliability refers to the trustworthiness of the content itself.[11] Digital information may become suspect and be rendered meaningless if a migration or some other action alters or corrupts the content or structure of a digital object, thus compromising its authenticity and/or reliability. The concept of collections sustainability is crucial to building strong, indispensable digital collections. In fact, many information professionals would recognize the concept as critical to fulfilling the library's very purpose.

28 Strategies for Sustaining Digital Libraries

Figure 2.1 illustrates how the components of this model of digital library sustainability – organization, technology, economic, and collections – work together horizontally to connect and overlap with each other, forming a complex of activities that sustain digital library activity. It also illustrates how the sustainability model components interact and function vertically, from the single institution level and upward through the multi-institutional consortial level, to the larger nonprofit management entities, and the even more expansive national and international partnerships.

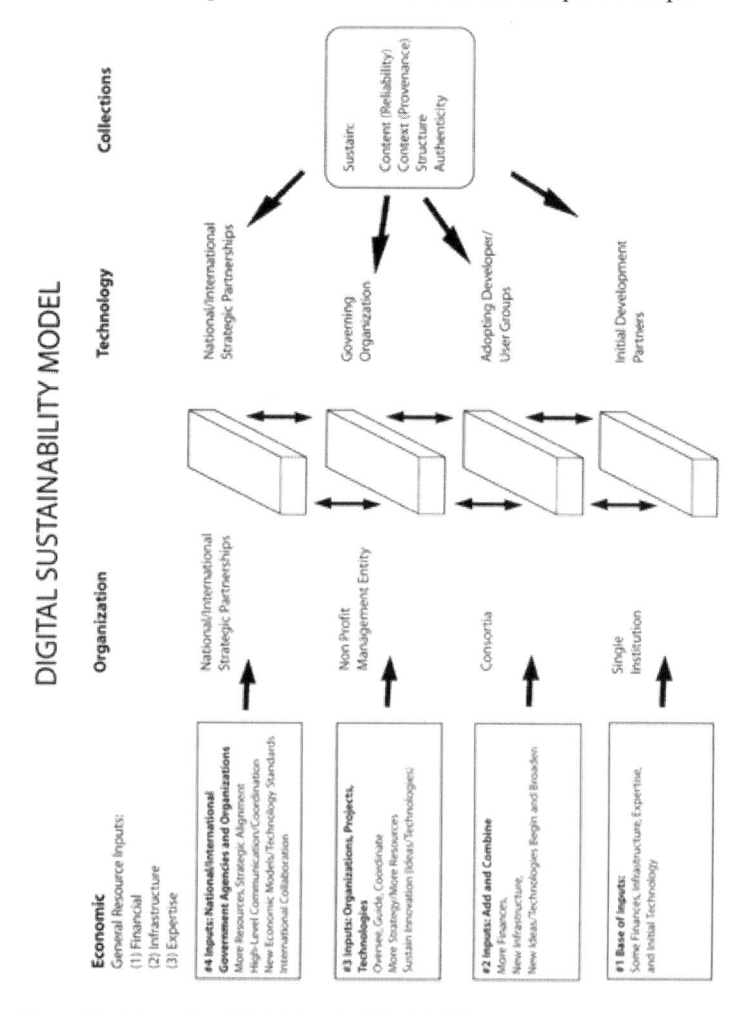

Figure 2.1: Schematic of Digital Sustainability Model.

CASE STUDY: THE METAARCHIVE COOPERATIVE

Background

The MetaArchive Cooperative formed in 2004 as the result of collaborative efforts among six university research libraries and archives. Since that time, it has worked to establish a solid strategy for archiving copies of content in secure, distributed locations. The Cooperative formed under the leadership of Emory University, and includes the following founding members: the Georgia Institute of Technology, Virginia Polytechnic Institute and State University, Florida State University, Auburn University, and the University of Louisville. At the time of the Cooperative's formation, concurrent digital preservation practices primarily consisted of geographically and institutionally homogeneous replication of content by host institutions. This approach leaves content at the mercy of the institution's technical infrastructure anomalies and vulnerable to destruction through both manmade and natural disasters.

Using leading software for distributed digital replication (the LOCKSS system from Stanford University), the MetaArchive Cooperative established in 2004 the first of its MetaArchive preservation networks, a *distributed* means of replicating digital archives.[12] This approach provides the geographic and institutional heterogeneity needed to safeguard each institution's digital collections. The Cooperative achieves redundancy through distribution of all content over at least six geographically dispersed servers by utilizing the backbone of the Internet2 Abilene network and the local connections of the Southern Crossroads (SoX) network consortium and the Mid-Atlantic Crossroads (MAX) network consortium.[13]

The MetaArchive Cooperative formed out of Emory University's MetaScholar Initiative. The Initiative has engaged in activities such as the MetaCombine Project, a multi-institutional project to provide access to scholarly information and services via OAI-PMH, and the related SouthComb Cyberinfrastructure for Scholars Project to produce a comprehensive scholarly portal and discovery service for research materials related to the cultures and histories of the U.S. South.[14,15] Several of the institutions involved in the MetaScholar Initiative formed the MetaArchive Cooperative to address issues related to the preservation of digital archives. Once the MetaArchive Cooperative was initiated, its steering committee members began investing time and energy to determine how they would sustain the Cooperative's organizational model, its technology, and its services. The digital sustainability model described above has helped to guide and develop the MetaArchive Cooperative's specific steps toward sustainability.

METAARCHIVE COOPERATIVE – ORGANIZATION SUSTAINABILITY

To shape organization sustainability, the MetaArchive Cooperative developed a relationship with the Library of Congress (LC), through its National Digital Information Infrastructure and Preservation Program (NDIIPP).[16] In October 2004, NDIIPP awarded the MetaArchive Cooperative with one of its eight original digital preservation partnerships. Collaborating with LC/NDIIPP gave the MetaArchive Cooperative access to a wide variety of resources and placed its work within the context of a national digital preservation agenda. Through NDIIPP, the MetaArchive Cooperative has access to LC's digital preservation partners and their approaches to similar issues, as well as access to expertise within LC itself, which is a great resource.

LC/NDIIPP has contributed to the MetaArchive Cooperative's organization sustainability on several levels. It has provided significant funding for Cooperative's growth, and has served as a catalyst, prompting the MetaArchive Cooperative to organize itself, its technology, and its services. NDIIPP has helped to provide the MetaArchive Cooperative with organizational and economic grounding. This support has helped the MetaArchive Cooperative achieve the positive position of considering its long-term viability and sustainability.

As part of the Cooperative's work with NDIIPP, the project group wrote and adopted a Cooperative Charter and Membership Agreement to govern the relationship between its members.[17] As one of the four major deliverables to LC in its initial project, these documents have themes and concepts that are generalizable to other consortia that embark on distributed digital preservation programs.

The Charter defines the MetaArchive Cooperative and its mission. Specifically, it establishes:

1. What types of members comprise the MetaArchive Cooperative:

a. *Sustaining Members* – develop and test the MetaArchive's preservation network technology and operate a preservation node
b. *Preservation Members* – operate a preservation node, ingest collections from member institutions, and make the node available for testing
c. *Contributing Members* – cultural memory institutions that possess digital content to preserve via the MetaArchive Cooperative's preservation networks. They contribute fees for this service and do not operate a node

2. How the MetaArchive Cooperative is organized and governed and how its members communicate:

   a. Through a committee-driven system, which includes steering, content, preservation, and technical committees
   b. With individual representatives from member institutions serving terms on the committees (This ensures broad participation in governance and operations)

3. What cooperative services the MetaArchive Cooperative offers its members in the digital preservation area:

   a. network development and maintenance
   b. content ingestion and retrieval
   c. format migration
   d. digital collection disaster recovery
   e. digital preservation network consulting
   f. LOCKSS services

The Charter also includes technical specifications for the MetaArchive Cooperative's preservation networks that Sustaining and Preservation members must follow and a Membership Agreement. The nexus of organization sustainability is the co-joining of the MetaArchive members, beginning with the initial six research libraries, which lays the foundation for growth as we extend membership opportunities to additional institutions. The Cooperative Charter is a product of this nexus.

In 2006, the founders of the MetaArchive Cooperative began to look beyond the LC/NDIIPP partnership and the Cooperative

Charter to further ensure its organizational sustainability. Three aspects have been considered: (1) the continuing need for financial resources, (2) the desire to continue integrating the MetaArchive Cooperative work with other digital projects that may inform its future development, and (3) the need for an economically efficient and catalytic structure to bring these two items about. Hence, the Cooperative determined that it would benefit by establishing a nonprofit management entity to host and guide its operations. Named the Educopia Institute, this nonprofit, founded in 2006, provides oversight of the Cooperative and other future digital projects.[18] It provides a low-cost, low-overhead conduit for completing those digital library and scholarly communications projects that will advance the cyberinfrastructure for research, teaching, and learning in our contemporary digital era.

Educopia's board of directors is discussing several new and potentially MetaArchive-related partnerships that might help construct this "cooperative educational cyberinfrastructure." The NSF defines cyberinfrastructure as:

> ... the distributed computer, information and communication technologies combined with the personnel and integrating components that provide a long-term platform to empower the modern scientific research endeavor.[19]

The Educopia Institute is putting a "higher education spin" on the meaning of cyberinfrastructure. The NSF report *Revolutionizing Science and Engineering through Cyberinfrastructure: Report of the National Science Foundation Advisory Panel on Cyberinfrastructure* (2003), introduced the paradigm known as "cyberinfrastructure." Three years later, humanities and social science scholars followed with *Our Cultural Commonwealth: The Final Report of the American Council of Learned Societies Commission on Cyberinfrastructure for the Humanities & Social Sciences* (2006). The latter report asserts that "effective cyberinfrastructure for the humanities and social sciences will allow scholars to focus their intellectual and scholarly energies on the issues that engage them, and to be effective users of new media and new technologies."[20] The Educopia Institute intends to continue the work called for in these seminal reports, acknowledging that all scholarly activities – teaching, researching, learning, and knowledge transfer through scholarly communications – need a rational and strategic cyberinfrastructure, regardless of whether these activities take place in the science, engineering, humanities, or social science fields. The Educopia Institute will generate technology projects that support this overall mission and goal.

Much work has taken place to grow the MetaArchive Cooperative into a sustainable organization. The four levels of organization building (institution, consortium, nonprofit management entity, and national/international strategic partner) should result in a dynamic organization that productively addresses distributed digital preservation issues.

MetaArchive Cooperative – Technology Sustainability

As it develops and sustains its technological infrastructure, the MetaArchive Cooperative is following the emerging sustainability model. The steps involved include: (1) assembling initial technology development members, (2) broadening the base of development members and initiating user groups, (3) establishing a governing organization that coordinates and sustains the developer and user groups, and (4) aligning these with national and international strategic partners. Since the MetaArchive technology is based upon existing open source software – LOCKSS – the technology path has been clear: support the development and maintenance of the LOCKSS software through the LOCKSS Alliance. Alliance membership is mandatory for all the MetaArchive Cooperative's Sustaining and Preservation members.

In 2004, the MetaArchive Cooperative anticipated adapting the software and either altering or adding code to the core LOCKSS software to utilize it with digital collections that are different in character from serialized material such as e-journals (e.g., archival collections, digital exhibits, and so on). Thus far, one application has been developed and added to LOCKSS: the MetaArchive Cooperative's conspectus database, which has been offered back to the LOCKSS community as an original contribution to the software. The conspectus contains the content and structure of the metadata schema developed by the Cooperative. It provides organization and control over the digital collections sustained within the MetaArchive Cooperative's preservation networks. While there are some differences when applying LOCKSS to a private network like the MetaArchive Cooperative's preservation networks, we have discovered that the fundamentals of LOCKSS work properly. The MetaArchive Cooperative's preservation networks were the first Private LOCKSS Networks (PLN) in use. In fact, there is much interest in developing PLNs today. This experience illustrates our general approach to technology sustainability – continually embedding an organization and its projects into other organizations and their projects – weaving a tapestry of interdependency.

The LOCKSS Alliance represents a technology sustainability strategy for the LOCKSS software. Emory University began the relationship as an early LOCKSS development partner with Stanford University. Georgia Tech became an early adopter, joining the Alliance immediately, and became involved in five LOCKSS-based projects. Both the LOCKSS Alliance and the MetaArchive Cooperative bring expertise and financial resources to advance LOCKSS. The MetaArchive Cooperative is interested in furthering LOCKSS technical development by integrating additional technologies, such as the Typed Object Model framework for format emulation.[21] There are plans to incorporate a framework for automated metadata generation as well.[22] Hence, it is a symbiotic relationship between the two consortia. The strategy of embedding the MetaArchive Cooperative into other strategic coalitions will yield further collaborative opportunities to develop, sustain, and integrate digital preservation technologies within the MetaArchive Cooperative's preservation networks.

MetaArchive Cooperative – Economic Sustainability

The MetaArchive Cooperative, like most consortial digital library projects, is concerned about its future economic viability. Our primary goal is building technological, organizational, and service models that are affordable and effective. The larger goal is to disseminate our digital preservation model and make it affordable for medium-sized cultural memory institutions. There are several layers of economic activity supporting the Cooperative. These follow the emerging model of interdependency to sustain digital libraries.

First, the six founding university members contributed resources to form the Cooperative. Economically, they have provided a base of infrastructure from which to operate. Server rooms, labor time, knowledge from expert personnel, and network connectivity are supplied and will be sustained as base contributions from each Cooperative member. The Cooperative began expanding its membership in the Fall of 2007, first welcoming its initial international partner, Hull University (UK). Each new institution that joins MetaArchive will bring its own resources to the Cooperative, including server management; collection development expertise; digital collections; and interests in developing the technology, organizational model, and services. This continued but controlled growth of members and investment should provide the economic foundation to ensure basic operations.

The strategic partnership with LC/NDIIPP assists economic sustainability primarily through funding. This currently provides for hardware as well as project-dedicated staff that perform a variety of technical and nontechnical activities. However, it also facilitates sustainability conversations within its "birds of a feather" discussion groups, comprised of its digital preservation partners. NDIIPP has a consultant, Paul Courant of the University of Michigan, who participates in meetings and projects regarding economic sustainability for digital preservation. Thus, NDIIPP helps the Cooperative by providing access to economic sustainability "know-how" residing with the other digital preservation partners as well as in other organizations currently working with LC, such as the NSF and their joint research program called Digital Archiving and Long-Term Preservation (DIGARCH). LC/NDIIPP also works with their U.K. counterpart, the Joint Information Systems Committee (JISC), through workshops and conferences that bring together the NDIIPP- and JISC-funded project principal investigators. Seeking strategic opportunities to align programs and projects with national and international initiatives is becoming increasingly important to generate revenues. Several countries are taking a centralized approach to funding (e.g., the UK with JISC and the Digital Curation Centre, and Australia with the Australian Partnership for Sustainable Repositories [APSR]).[23] The U.S. is beginning to do so as well with NDIIPP.

The nonprofit management entity, the Educopia Institute, generates revenues from other funders and through synergies with partners and related projects. Monies from NDIIPP and from its initial Sustaining Member's membership fees helped provide for its founding and early activities. This nonprofit will identify other digital library- and e-scholarship-related projects to undertake, work toward locating funding, and, where appropriate, integrate the MetaArchive Cooperative into these projects. In relation to the MetaArchive, the Educopia Institute functions like a holding company, providing general oversight and a low-cost, low-overhead financial management role. There will be a mix of projects, and some will naturally link to the MetaArchive Cooperative. While a relationship to the Cooperative is not required, new projects may be leveraged with the technologies and organizational relationships already established therein.

Service and consulting fees provide additional revenue streams that contribute to maintenance of the Preservation Network. We offer a range of services to cultural memory institutions. First, the Cooperative provides fee-based services to contributing members to preserve their digital content. The fees support the Preservation Network's maintenance costs. Second, there are consortia of cultural memory institutions developing their own PLNs. Projects currently underway include: the Network of Alabama Academic Libraries, Michigan state-affiliated public universities, and the Arizona State Library, Archives and Public Records network. We work in a consulting capacity with many of these emergent PLNs.

While much remains to be determined regarding the MetaArchive Cooperative's economic sustainability, we are acutely aware of the need to focus on this issue. In the first years of the MetaArchive Cooperative, we have begun to address its economic needs. The current progress is positive, and Cooperative members look forward to sharing with and learning from other consortia who are experimenting with new models and activities relating to economic sustainability.

MetaArchive Cooperative – Collections Sustainability

Collections sustainability involves developing strategies to ensure that the defining qualities of an information object persist. The authentic nature of digital collections, the reliability of their content, and the ability to trace an object's handling and use over time and across technologies are paramount to maintaining the value, usefulness, and quality of digital collections. Through format emulation technology, LOCKSS' built-in routines for checking a file's technical integrity, and specific metadata, the MetaArchive Cooperative has taken marked steps toward sustaining its collections' original character.[24]

Incorporating format emulation tools will allow the Preservation Network to generate currently renderable digital versions without altering the original collection. In 2005, Jantz and Giarlo described a digital preservation archive as consisting of the "digital original and digital derivatives" resulting from format migration.[25] This approach allows the original collection with all its defining characteristics to exist unaltered. In addition, as format migration and emulation technologies improve, creating new renderings from the original digital collections will improve. Ensuring authenticity and reliability are two reasons the MetaArchive Cooperative is seeking to incorporate this type of software tool. Through metadata, the MetaArchive Cooperative is documenting the provenance of the collections preserved in its network. Some of the metadata fields in its conspectus database provide information about the creation, use, and handling of the digital collections and how those actions have affected them.[26] Fields like "Custodial History," "Creator," "Format Characteristics," "Accrual Periodicity," "Accrual Period," and "Manifestation" provide this meta-information. Information in these fields may indicate whether collections have been altered, changed, or possibly corrupted, as well as how, when, and why changes have occurred. The Cooperative plans to sustain its collections' original characteristics through these and other steps.

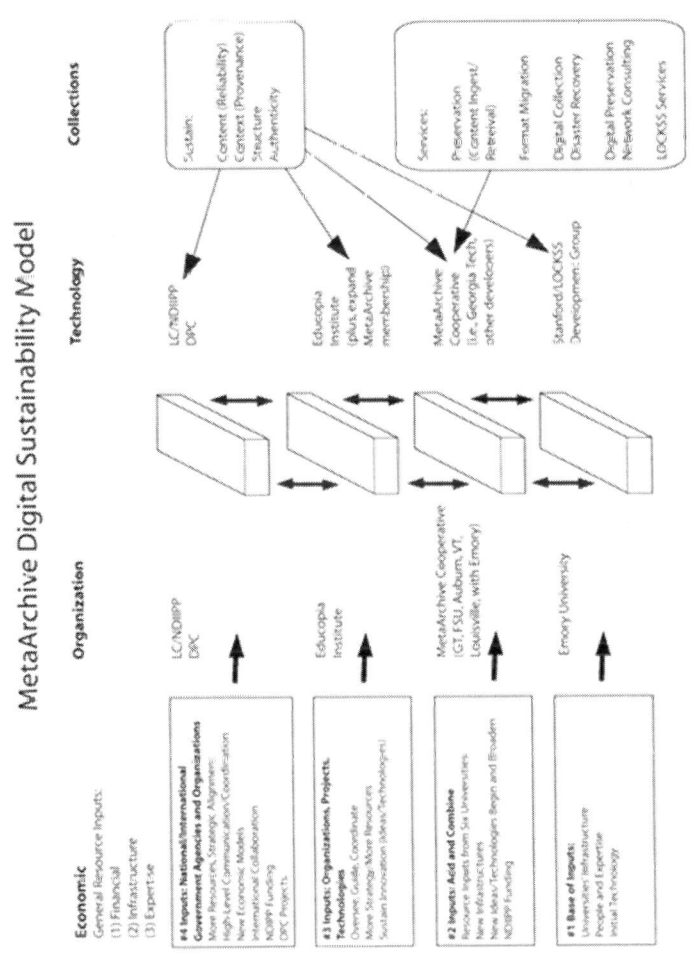

Figure 2.2. Digital Sustainability Model as Applied to MetaArchive

CONCLUSION – AN EMERGING MODEL FOR SUSTAINING DIGITAL LIBRARIES

Applying the sustainability model described to the work of the MetaArchive Cooperative should result in a dynamic organization well equipped to address digital preservation networking issues. Figure 2.2 illustrates the digital sustainability model for the MetaArchive Cooperative. As it guides other digital library activities, such as the development of metadata and the creation of search and resource discovery technology, this model should provide similar results as the core consortium networks, giving the Cooperative access to a strong social network. The need to build such relationships with institutions, consortia, organizations, high-level strategic partners, and other entities has intensified dramatically. Weaving this tapestry of interdependency will advance digital library programs and spur innovation and knowledge sharing within our international community. These are the next steps to improving digital library sustainability – building additional layers of organizational linkages, interlacing more entities to weave a larger, more diverse tapestry, and improving the richness of the social organizational network. We see this phenomenon occurring generally in our global society, in business, and in education. Author Thomas L. Friedman provides this insight:

> In the flat world, more and more business will be done through collaboration...the more the flattening of the world connects all the knowledge pools together, the more new specialties will be spawned, and the more innovation will come from putting these specialties together in new and different combinations.[27]

Friedman's observations are words to live by for the digital library/archives community as it strives to collaborate, accelerate human innovation, and disseminate new discoveries through learning, research, and scholarship on a global scale.

NOTES

1. Paul Arthur Berkman, "Once in a Hundred Generations," In *Strategies for Sustaining Digital Libraries*, eds. Katherine Skinner and Martin Halbert (Atlanta: Emory University Digital Library Publications, 2008), p. 11.

2. Minutes of the CENDI Principals and Alternates Meeting, National Science Foundation, Ballston Virginia, January 4, 2005. http://cendi.dtic.mil/minutes/pa_0105.html

3. See L.C. Freeman. *The Development of Social Network Analysis: A Study in the Sociology of Science* (Vancouver: Empirical Press,

2004). See also Everett Rogers. *Diffusion of Innovations*. (New York: The Free Press, 1962).
4. See http://www.metaarchive.org.
5. Milward, H. Brinton and Keith G. Provan. *A Manager's Guide to Choosing and Using Collaborative Networks* (2006): 8. http://www.businessofgovernment.org/main/publications/grant_reports/details/index.asp?gid=195.
6. Open source software is defined as software where the source code is open and available to people, where any additionally developed code is added back into the original source code, and the software is openly redistributed. See http://www.opensource.org/docs/def_print.php.
7. See also http://www.redhat.com/about/mission/opensource.html
8. See http://www.DSpace.org, http://www.LOCKSS.org, http://www.fedora.info, http://www.sakaiproject.org, http://shibboleth.internet2.edu, www.openarchives.org
9. Duranti, Luciana. "Reliability and Authenticity: The Concepts and Their Implications." *Archivaria*, 39 (Spring 1995): 5-10.
10. Peter Bunerman, Khanna Sanjeev, and Ta Wang-Chiew. "Data Provenance: Some Basic Issues." In *FST TCS 2000: Foundations of Software Technology and Theoretical Computer Science: 20th Conference, New Delhi, India, December 2000, Proceedings*, 87-93.
11. Shelby Sanett and Eun Park. "Authenticity as a Requirement of Preserving Digital Data and Records," *IASSIST Quarterly* (Winter 1999 / Spring 2000): 15-18.
12. See The LOCKSS Program, (http://lockss.stanford.edu/).
13. See the Abilene Map (http://www.internet2.edu/resources/AbileneMap.pdf), Southern Crossroads, (http://www.sox.net/), and Mid-Atlantic Crossroads (http://www.maxgigapop.net/).
14. See http://www.MetaCombine.org
15. See http://www.metascholar.org/SouthComb/
16. See http://www.digitalpreservation.gov
17. See http://www.metaarchive.org/pdfs/MetaArchiveCharter_0707.pdf
18. See http://educopia.org
19. Revolutionizing Science and Engineering through Cyberinfrastructure. Report of the National Science Foundation Advisory Panel on Cyberinfrastructure, February 3, 2003. (Arlington, VA: National Science Foundation): 1-2. See also http://www.nsf.gov/od/lpa/news/03/pr0318.htm.
20. See http://www.acls.org/cyberinfrastructure/cyber_what_is.htm.

21. See http://tom.library.upenn.edu/.
22. For resources on automated metadata generation tools, see the University of North Carolina's Metadata Research Center, automated metadata generation applications at: http://ils.unc.edu/mrc/amega.
23. See JISC at http://www.jisc.ac.uk/ and the APSR at http://www.apsr.edu.au/.
24. David S. H. Rosenthal, Thomas Robertson, Tom Lipkis, Vicky Reich, and Seth Morabito. "Requirements for Digital Preservation Systems: A Bottom Up Approach," *D-Lib Magazine* 11 (November 2005). http://www.dlib.org/dlib/november05/rosenthal/11rosenthal.html.
25. Ronald Jantz and Michael J. Giarlo. Digital Preservation: Architecture and Technology for Trusted Digital Repositories. *D-Lib Magazine* 11:6 (June 2005). http://www.dlib.org/dlib/june05/jantz/06jantz.html.
26. See: http://www.metaarchive.org/pdfs/conspectus_md_2005.html)
27. Thomas L. Friedman. *The World is Flat: A Brief History of the Twenty-First Century.* (New York: Farrar, Straus and Giroux, 2006): 353.

What Is This New Devilry?
Digital Libraries and the Fate of Faculty Scholarship and Publishing

Bradley Daigle (University of Virginia)

Abstract: Recent trends in scholarly activity, loosely defined as digital scholarship, call for new strategies for the support and preservation of the scholarly record. Digital libraries can function in many capacities, including information repository, management tool, and publishing service. Linking these activities to the academic mission of the institution as well as the development of a solid cyberinfrastructure is critical to the continued relevance of libraries within higher education.

SCHOLARSHIP: PAST AND PRESENT.

I am reminded in writing this of the time I watched the first episode in Peter Jackson's *Lord of the Rings* trilogy. The scene I have in mind depicts a beleaguered, heroic crew running about in the dark bowels of the Mines of Moria. After having encountered the ancient remains of a battle in which the "good guys" were killed to the last, it is not difficult for Frodo and his pals to visualize how they may suffer the same fate. Just when it seems that things could not get any worse, they sense a new, grander, looming danger. It is at this juncture that the ill-fated Boromir utters in restrained despair: "What is this new devilry?"

There are many parallels that I could draw from this vignette to our current state of affairs within higher education and digital libraries and scholarship.[1] For example, the disturbing encounter among the ancient battle remains serves as a grim reminder that past methodologies and strategies – born of high valor and at times, desperation – do not always have happy outcomes. One could also conclude that history can repeat itself, though not always with the same results.

Having escaped that particular cul-de-sac, the heroes are beset by adversaries on all sides. It is noteworthy that they are able to dispatch known enemies despite grave odds. However, it is the introduction of this new form of "devilry" that is to tear their fellowship asunder. Unable to grasp and defend against this latest nemesis, it is only through extreme self-sacrifice that they are able to derail their greatest foe to date.

Now, I am taking for granted that most readers have seen or at least read *Lord of the Rings: The Fellowship of the Ring*, an assumption that puts my extended metaphor at some risk. However, I do not think that most readers will lose the overarching point that is being made: there is a renewed, beleaguered feeling that scholarship struggles valiantly against – that is, its own history and the new tides of change that swell around it. Any new methodology that does not fit within the current framework, particularly one that threatens to sink the entire structure, is met with anything from skepticism to exasperation, from giddiness to despondency. New approaches to how research is carried out must struggle against centuries of inertia.[2]

The purpose of this discussion is to scrutinize the relationship between new forms of scholarship and the new forms of library environments needed to support it. Digital scholarship can be viewed as a new type of devilry – it is difficult to define, complex and rapidly shifting, and certainly very resource intensive from a support perspective. Historical perspectives reveal how much the terrain has changed in academe. The University of Virginia (UVa) Library has been working with faculty to support large-scale information management and dissemination both past and future but the road has not been an easy one. Libraries need to act decisively by forming strategic partnerships to support new forms of research and develop new environments to manage and "publish" this content. If they do not, then they will have lost an opportunity to provide much needed leadership in this particular area within higher education.

At their very core, libraries have remained fundamentally unchanged for centuries. As an institution, the Library has been highly successful in promulgating its mission and identity across cultures and generations – a reality due largely to the manner of scholarship it supports. This does not mean that libraries have prospered unabated and revel in the untold wealth such determinism can bring. It is quite the opposite. Libraries are constantly under siege by the myriad forces of their mission: to collect, organize, and make information accessible to others. Over the centuries – and more recently this activity has become highly condensed – libraries have been recreating themselves internally in response to environmental changes while leaving their external "face" relatively clear and unchanged. Similar to libraries, the apparatus of humanities scholarship has changed very little in its general methodology over the centuries. In other words, for both, the specific discoveries have had a dramatic impact within the profession but the overall institution can be said to have changed very little.[3]

Traditionally, humanities scholarship is an end that has been attainable by an individual on almost entirely that individual's own terms. In other words, it is an individual contribution ambitiously pointed towards the "greater good" of all scholarship in a given field or fields. To a certain extent, the framework that supports this model is still very much in place. Libraries still collect materials related to humanities scholarship activity, these collections are still managed and stewarded, and they are available to scholars for consultation as well. In modern terms, scholarship is the main end product of higher education academic departments. This activity has been undertaken for centuries but significantly increased since the passing of the GI Bill in the middle of last century.[4] However, there are severely mitigating factors that are now poised in direct opposition to the way things have been done historically. For example within the last few years, the sheer volume of research materials has grown at a staggering rate. This can be attributed to the cumulative effects of collecting as well as the massive output from the digital production cycle of academe and industry. Individual scholars now have to rely more heavily on the external management and arrangement of these voluminous materials in order to do their work. Research becomes reliant upon the available tools for each scholar and the training services that support and deliver them. Finally, there are economic trends within the academic profession conspiring against scholarship as we know it.[5] In fact, parameters both within academe and the free market are now shifting with the increased use of new forms of scholarship – in particular digital forms – that inflict broad tectonic shifts in the mission of libraries.

We have looked at how research and scholarship have largely worked together historically, forming a solid bond within higher education that was mutually supportive. Today, as I alluded to above, libraries are experiencing a massive transformation. This is occurring in part as a reaction to new forms of scholarship and research. However, this time we are changing from within and without, molting into our newer, digital form. At heart, it is the same institution following many of the same guiding principles but in many fundamental ways we are no longer recognizable in our new appearance. "Digital libraries" and "digital scholarship" are both newer forms of old institutions. They borrow from their antecedents and are yet evolving on a much shorter cycle. But these shifts in how scholars approach their research and scholarship are not unilateral, as some scholars are adopting digital services, others cling to traditional print sources, and still others readily use and produce both.

Humanities scholarship in particular has been slow to resist the inertia of its historical traditions. Noted Civil War historian and early adopter of digital scholarship, Ed Ayers, states: "While the texts of their trade are becoming rapidly available anywhere, anytime, humanities scholars, who might have much to gain from digital media's potential to spread their scholarship, remain firmly committed to traditional forms" (quoted in Brogan 2005). This feeling speaks to a growing wedge between generations of humanities scholars and the libraries that support them. Brogan's essay continues in the same vein: "Recent PhDs interviewed for this report bear witness to even harsher judgments by established faculty in English Departments about the value of digital media: it is irrelevant scholarship, a matter of indifference to them, or not even in their consciousness" (Brogan 2005).[6] Whose responsibility is it to bridge this divide between scholarship and support in libraries?

Clearly, libraries need to adapt to changing needs as well. California Digital Library's Daniel Greenstein states in *The Chronicle of Higher Education*'s technology forum in a panel titled "The Library as Search Engine" that library traditional public catalogues need to change: "These cataloging systems are discovery systems that are basically designed according to a conceptual framework developed 40 years ago, and they do not provide what people now expect from searches" (*Chronicle* 2007a). As we shift our focus to the relationship between digital scholarship and digital libraries it becomes essential to understand their powerful binding agent: cyberinfrastructure.

Cyberinfrastructure has certainly been around for years. However, for the sake of this discussion, I will speak to its broad bearing on digital scholarship, particularly in the humanities. Director of the

National Science Foundation Arden L. Bement refers to cyberinfrastructure as "a comprehensive phenomenon that involves the creation, dissemination, preservation, and application of knowledge." It "encompasses a diverse array of interrelated social, economic, and legal factors, everything from norms of practice and rules to incentives and constraints that shape individual and collective action" (Bement 2007). These elements form an essential infrastructure upon which many services can be built. It should be stable and reliable so that innovation and experimentation build upon its foundation, filtering down to effect the cyberinfrastructure below but also the environment in which these types of activities can take place. It is critical to both supporting and sustaining digital scholarship.

The cost for implementing a successful cyberinfrastructure is significant. The many factors involved in how libraries and universities support the needs of the faculty make a single model unlikely. This is where partnerships are needed: with IT units, consortia, colleges, and organizations. For example, a 2006 National Science Foundation and Association of Research Libraries workshop looked into the broad issues surrounding the proper stewardship of digital files.[7] Not surprisingly, the participants of this group explored issues related to the need for collaborative partnerships that will build the "...necessary *infrastructure development* to support digital data; and the need for *sustainable economic models* to supporting long-term stewardship" of digital data for "the nation's cyberinfrastructure" (italics theirs) (ARL 2006). It is clear that for libraries to support the longevity of scholarship and its dissemination, we need to better understand what digital scholarship means.

What is digital scholarship with respect to new trends in libraries? I see digital scholarship as a method of scholarly communication, research, and exchange of ideas that employs modern forms of technology, in particular, those forms of technology maintained within an institution's cyberinfrastructure. The American Council of Learned Society's report on cyberinfrastructure entitled, *Our Cultural Heritage*, boldly indicates that the authors believe that this form of scholarship is the future of all scholarship (ACLS 2006). This report firmly places humanities and social sciences research at the forefront of digital scholarship. In fact, they offer multiple strategies for how higher education should support such activities. In many ways, such reports highlight some of the primary challenges for libraries today: namely, to develop a methodology for supporting the disparate activities that make up digital scholarship. Core library services need to be employed in order to support digital scholarship in a manner that is appropriate to the institution's mission. These can be collecting strategies, organizational models, as well as developing new tools for managing this scholarship. That said, this digital scholarship requires a new form of library environment – one that is adaptable and extensible, one that properly adjusts to changing technologies. Enter the digital library.

Differing perspectives on what comprises a digital library form a large part of our professional literature. Books, articles, and conferences are entirely devoted to adding to our lexicon of library-technology word play. Archive, repository, library, and digital library: such terms tend to blur with such ubiquitous use. Let us say, for the sake of this argument, that a digital library is just another layer of services built into and on top of an institution's cyberinfrastructure. In one case, a digital library can serve as an institutional repository of all digitized materials, in whatever form, bound loosely by policies and management tools. In this example, a digital library can be managed in part by librarians, but also perhaps by the individual users – or any combination thereof. Librarians, technologists, administrators, and a host of others need to be involved in the deployment and maintenance of such a library but do not necessarily need to be the sole arbiters of its content. The operative word in any definition of library should be "managed" or "managing" in some form. An archive, or repository can exist as a bank of storage that houses files but it is the intentionality of such storage and use from a broad perspective that is required in this scenario. However, use of the term *library* implies that there exists an overarching strategy for such storage and use.

Another iteration of a digital library depicts an environment strictly managed by librarians and technologists – working together to blend the possibilities of digital tools with the emerging forms of scholarship that faculty create. This should be an environment that balances standards and innovation. It is my belief that, in some form, digital libraries are our main hope for sustaining digital scholarship. In the future, digital libraries could house the entire research and intellectual output of a university's faculty and students as well as discrete collections created by faculty and preserved as part of the library's mission. For now, a digital library needs to grow in an environment that has invested substantially in its cyberinfrastructure because that environment needs to be reliable and "trustworthy" in the Lynchian sense.[8] Library technologies and services need to support the creation of digital scholarship; digital libraries need to sustain that scholarship. This is a critical nuance in the relationship between digital scholarship and digital libraries. The "supporting" does not need to necessarily plug into the "sustaining" in every case, but there must be a level of intentionality behind such decision-making policies.

In fact, one might need multiple repositories as well as a digital library: in a recent NSF/ARL report the findings state that: "Responsibility for the stewardship of digital information should be vested in distributed collections and repositories that recognize the heterogeneity of the data while ensuring the potential for federation and interoperability" (ARL 2006). It is unlikely that one single motorway can hold all the "traffic" that is created by an institution but it is critical that these systems interrelate and interoperate. Separate solutions for digital output may in fact be required but they should not be isolated from each other – not unlike universities that have "main" libraries and branch libraries within their entire library system (but hopefully a single OPAC). It seems that when this concept of multiple solutions is translated into the digital realm, the potential for anxiety increases by relative orders of magnitude, especially when one considers the need for digital preservation and access.[9] There must always be a balance between existing and emerging standards. The tension that pulls on either side of this spectrum is what digital scholarship enhances in every element of its development and implementation. Digital library development often struggles with this tension and it is for that very reason that we need to employ multiple strategies for sustaining faculty digital scholarship.

What is happening at the University of Virginia?

Currently, UVa is undergoing a massive transformation of its legacy digital content. Early faculty adopters have delved deeply into the depths of digital scholarship. In the early years of digital scholarship, the support model was sporadic and uneven. By the mid 1990s, the digital library landscape at UVa was primarily project-based, relatively unknown (both internally and externally) except by the faculty involved in their creation, and were rarely integrated with one another to form an organic and coherent collection. Hundreds and thousands of digital orphans were created, doomed to have their orbit slowly decay and be consigned to a technological oblivion. Each individual project had its idiosyncratic infrastructure, largely based upon whatever technology, tools, and services were available at the time it was proposed. It is very much a digital, phenomenological milieu, where scholarship was created in a "ready to hand" methodology that was self-absorbed in its own creative act more so than in its longevity.

However, this environment also had its exciting and positive side. Without a doubt, the mid 1990s was a time of massive exploration and creation of digital tools and objects. New ground was broken almost every day as faculty members rushed to try out new technologies and libraries struggled to keep up with a groundswell of activity previously unknown to them. It is only now, perhaps like Edward Bellamy's Julian West, that we see more clearly what was happening in this early evolutionary moment. Today, however, we are working to migrate this earlier content to more stable standards and to a more solid foundation. This is no small task: UVa is simultaneously migrating older content as well as developing new support models for new scholarship coming through the door.

Like many institutions, UVa Library struggles with the workload of managing and migrating legacy content along with the creation of new content. Digitizing activities are integrated in almost every facet of the institution both physically and philosophically. These voluminous activities threaten to strain the already tenuous hold libraries maintain on their digital services and support. One of the most important questions concerning the preservation of digital scholarship is: "How do scholars and librarians work together to ensure that resources created today will be available in the future?" (Marcum 2002).

One answer is given through the up-front service layer, which I call the "supporting" digital scholarship angle, and which can be tied directly to the services that a library establishes. This is the part of the cyberinfrastructure that consults with faculty to meet both their immediate and long-term needs for digital scholarship. The real work for sustaining digital scholarship happens through the development of digital libraries that deploy such scholarship. Sustaining digital scholarship is done through long-term preservation strategies, as well as "publishing" that research and maintaining its access. Planning in advance is critical: publishing and preservation should be forethoughts, not afterthoughts: "Librarians need to engage faculty in transforming scholarly communications at the beginning of the process" (Maloy 2006). If we do not actively engage and train our faculty to understand more fully the implications of their digital scholarship then we are doomed to repeat our legacy migration patterns. For the librarians and technologists who support digital library environments it is important that we capture the attention of those who are creating the content – before it is created – so as to guide that decision making process. This helps both librarians as stewards of the scholarship and the creators themselves as owners of their own intellectual property (Marcum 2002). These activities can run the range of services from a solid long-term view of preservation to the more immediate and necessary steps involved in digital curation.[10] So what are some specific strategies we can apply in this environment?

There are many possible approaches one can take to using a digital library environment to sustain scholarship (and itself be sustained). As I mentioned above, UVa has a several staff members dedicated to sustaining digital scholarship. This group has been working for several years to map out solutions for legacy content to be added to our digital collections. Not surprisingly, there are mixed results in such efforts but I will outline the guiding principles by which we operate:

- Stage 1: Determine the scope of the scholarship as defined by the faculty member (for example).
- Stage 2: Collect and select the materials that comprise the digital scholarship.
- Stage 3: Assess or analyze the digital scholarship components.
- Stage 4: Develop and formalize agreements between parties.
- Stage 5: Implement service and procedural methods to formally ingest the digital scholarship into our digital library environment.
- Stage 6: Deliver via agreed upon method. This could also include "publishing" of the digital scholarship.

The first stage of the process deals with the consultation that is mentioned above. Provide a methodology and environment that is standards-based at its core but also adaptable to innovation. This is the balancing act between long-term support and innovative approaches to scholarship that have not yet become standards.[11]

There are some basic principles for the service-end to consider:

- Staffing
- Equipment
- Formats
- Partnerships

Staffing may appear to be simply a question of "who does what" but in reality, it is far more complex. Handoffs both within and between units often result in bottlenecks and breakdowns. This is particularly true for those developing digital libraries. The staff that are dedicated to specific tasks need to understand where they fit into the overall picture of the support environment; otherwise disconnects will develop between the support services and the long-term sustaining services. Secondly, the formats that you support will depend largely upon which equipment you support. The need to balance what you need to archive because of intellectual value and what you can accomplish with available technology means that one must encourage faculty to use commonly accepted standards where appropriate for their projects so that their scholarship can later be migrated.[12] Digital libraries are not the sole destinations for materials created by libraries' digitization equipment, however, those that are selected to be supported in that manner need to draw upon the organizational strengths of such an environment, such as enhanced specifications (metadata, PPI resolution, annotations) and the aggregation power of a unified digital library environment.

Certainly having a team such as UVa's Sustaining Digital Scholarship group is essential to viewing such longitudinal service support. Digital libraries are but a part of such a landscape and should not be the only available option for delivering faculty-generated digital scholarship. The following illustration provides a general framework under development at the UVa Library. It depicts a general workflow as follows (Fig 1):

1. A user has a need for something to be digitally transformed (image, text, data, audio, video, etc.).
2. This user works directly with a public service staff member in the library who then organizes and submits the request for digitization via a specific request system (a combination of personal and technological) that logs, delivers, and tracks the request throughout the process.
3. A centralized digital management unit is used to vet the request for additional issues such as intellectual property concerns, scope of request, intended use. These decisions are guided by a broad set of policies and collection development practices as well as discussions with the public service staff member making the request for the faculty member.
    a. This centralized unit manages the entire process of content creation and delivery. Its current structure manages the workflows centrally, but the actual creation can occur across the university in a series of decentralized units dedicated to specific formats. It is also limited in the number of formats it currently supports but it is hoped that it will be able to expand over time.
    b. To handle economies of scale, a limited number of output formats are required based on the intended use (e.g. tiff vs. jpeg).
4. The intended use, timeframe, and scope of the request will be the primary factors in deciding which workflow is initiated for the request. If the purposes are deemed to be solely for access to the content then a less intensive workflow is required. For example, if the request needs several hundred images for a simple presentation then jpeg derivatives will be created.
5. The content will either be delivered into our digital library environment or separately on portable media (or both). The institutional repository is based on an overlapping infrastructure with the digital library, learning management system, digital tools for object manipulation, and a separate faculty project server environment. Each of these instances can pull the files into a specific

environment and apply a new or universal suite of actions on the objects (aggregate in a website, deploy in experimental tools, publish). The total environment should provide the capability to integrate tools, content, and services longitudinally while still providing the user with the ability to use materials in a space that is fairly flexible and built with an eye for deploying new technologies that could build upon this solid structure.

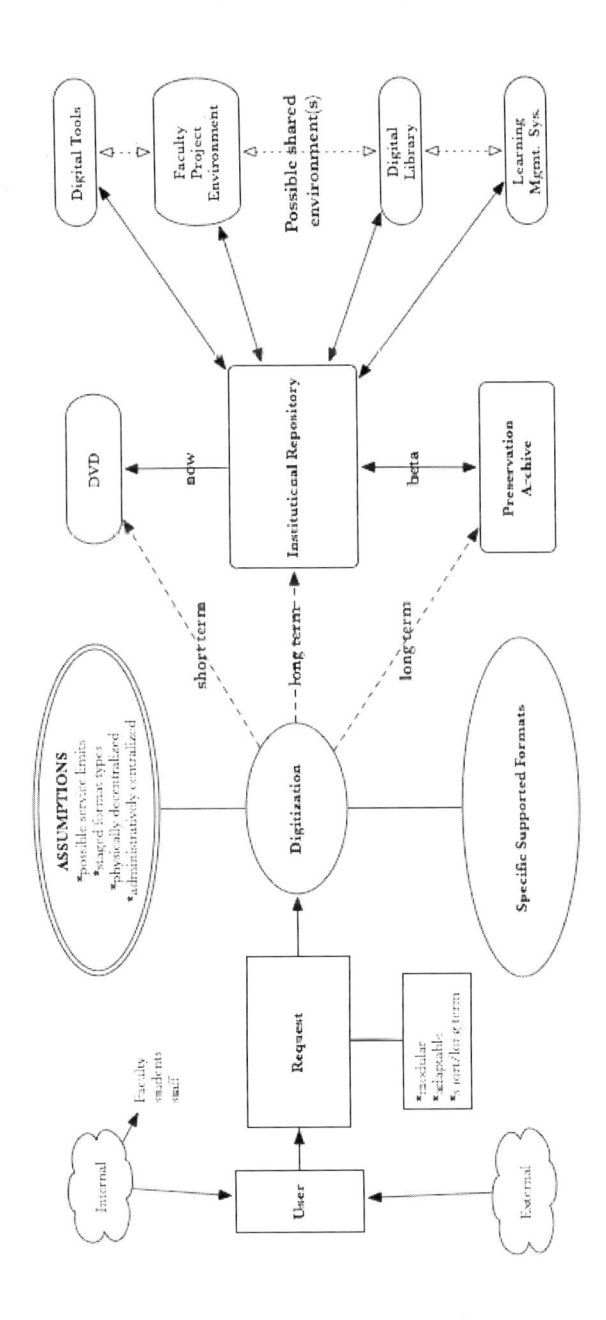

Figure 3.1: A high level sample model of a digital library environment.

This is a brief overview of what the UVa Library is rolling out in a series of stages. I expect that the underlying model of this system will remain constant, whereas the specifics that support and surround it will change. The environment needed for these activities is a basic element of cyberinfrastructure that is driving the support, creation, management, and delivery of digital scholarship within the university. A notable element of this scenario is that the library cannot achieve this vision on its own. Strategic partnerships with the university's information technology group, the university press, and faculty members, among others, help to foster this development. The support system is so vast and deep that it is very unlikely one single unit within a university would be able to implement such a system in its entirety. In this scenario we have built the beginnings of a solid support structure for managing digital objects and collecting digital scholarship. How do we make that content available to broad audiences? How do we give faculty more options for disseminating their research?

As mentioned earlier, publishing has historically been the vehicle for scholarship's dissemination. In the "traditional" model, faculty members conduct research and publish it in journals or monographs. These products are then purchased by libraries for long-term retention, preservation, and use. Slight variations on this model have been in practice for centuries and are not likely to end any time soon. However, this is no longer the only means for "publishing" in a digital environment. In fact, as Clifford Lynch recently notes: "Just because the existing scholarly publishing system has served the academy fairly well in the past doesn't mean that it has an intrinsic right to continue to exist in perpetuity" (Lynch 2006). One need not go into the intricacies of rising journal prices and diminishing market competition for journal vendors to believe that alternatives to the scholarly publishing model could be a market-healthy direction to pursue. How do new models of publishing digital scholarship merge with the realm of digital libraries? If one considers the above model useful – even in a rudimentary fashion – then it should be clear that developing a suite of "publishing" services to support faculty members is required. These services need to be aware of the different needs scholars have depending on where they are in their scholarly career. These can range from fee-based services to open source models. Digital libraries in academic settings should strive towards using open access standards to ensure that this information is freely available to as large an audience as possible. In fact, pursuing open access and free culture models is critical to keeping this material viable and real.[13]

Various digital publishing models are well suited to digital scholarship production. By its very nature, digital scholarship is frequently an iterative process with the end product changing over time. The idea of "versioning" is akin to editions in the publishing world; however it is much easier to version a work within a solid digital library environment. New forms of technology and communication will also drive new models of publishing digital scholarship. There needs to be a constant exchange between the scholars and the library services that support them. This will ensure the viability of the scholarship within an adapting infrastructure.

The main reason for pairing scholarship and digital libraries within higher education is the University's drive to make this scholarship widely available: "A cyberinfrastructure for humanities and social sciences must encourage interactions between the expert and the amateur, the creative artist and the scholar, the teacher and the student," stated the Cultural Commonwealth Report issued by ACLS in 2006. "It is not just the collection of data – digital or otherwise – that matters: at least as important is the activity that goes on around it, contributes to it, and eventually integrates with it." (ACLS 2006). Digital publishing needs to be built upon a structure whose design is to maintain and manage digital content. At UVa, we are still rolling out this structure. However, we are optimistic that faculty will be able to use this initial structure as a springboard for broader discussions of how such services can become attuned to the new methods of scholarly communication that they are exploring.

There are many good reasons to look at digital scholarship as a new form of devilry. It threatens to overwhelm and drown us in new service models and deeper management layers for curating digital objects, as just a few examples. Defining what cyberinfrastructure is and how it is an integral part of what libraries and researchers need is an excellent first step to where we need to go. Recent progress in digital library environments has allowed that infrastructure to grow as well. Further development is needed to ascertain what the long-term needs are within higher education for the "sustaining" of that research but those, too, are underway. Digital scholarship is bewitching in its seeming simplicity. But that clean exterior is built upon a complex set of relationships. It is also pulling libraries into the realm of publishing – a role that needs careful defining so as to differentiate what we do from our own university presses. If we do not work with strategic partners to develop the proper support environment for faculty research, we will have lost a major opportunity to demonstrate how relevant librarianship is today, perhaps more than it ever has been. Devilry, indeed; but at least with researchers and librarians working together on these new technologies, the fellowship has begun anew.

NOTES

1. At this point I feel I need to frame my discussion of "library" and "scholarship" to avoid any misinterpretations. For the purposes of this argument, the specific higher education institutions I have in mind are mostly research libraries in general and UVa specifically. With respect to scholarship, whereas I believe it happens at many levels and in many different places, I frame scholarship to be the end product of academic departments and the scholars they house. My particular scholarship bias is one that favors humanities research, although much of the discussion applies to scholarship from all disciplines.

2. Inertia has both positive and negatives aspects. From a physicist's standpoint, inertia is what keeps cars on the road during sharp turns, keeps us from spinning off the planet itself – these are good things. From an administrator's viewpoint, inertia is often used as a synonym for complacency – a retardant to any forward-thinking institution.

3. For an interesting overview of how research and the university interrelate as well as a thoughtful explication of where it should go, see James L. Duderstadt and Luc E. Weber's *Reinventing the Research University* (Duderstadt 2004).

4. For a few good overviews of the impact of the GI Bill of Rights see for example, Michael Bennett's *When Dreams Came True: The GI Bill and the Making of Modern America* (Brassey's 1996) and Suzanne Mettler's *Soldiers to Citizens: The GI Bill and the Making of the Greatest Generation* (Oxford 2005).

5. See the recent Modern Language Association Task Force's *Report on Tenure and Promotion* that was launched in 2004 "in response to widespread anxiety in the profession about ever-rising demands for research productivity and shrinking humanities lists by academic publishers, worries that forms of scholarship other than single-authored books were not being properly recognized, and fears that a generation of junior scholars would have significantly reduced chance of being tenured" (MLA pg. 4).

6. This fact is corroborated by the recent report on promotion and tenure put out by the Modern Language Association: "Even more troubling is the state of evaluation for digital scholarship, now an extensively used resource for scholars across the humanities: 40% of departments in doctorate granting institutions report no experience evaluating refereed articles in electronic format, and 65.7% report no experience evaluating monographs in electronic format." (MLA 2006)

7. This is the NSF and ARL workshop on "New Collaborative Relationships: Academic Libraries and the Digital Data Universe," held in September 2006.

8. See Clifford Lynch's article: "Institutional Repositories: Essential Infrastructure for Scholarship in the Digital Age." (Lynch 2003).

9. Deanna Marcum states in "Preservation of Scholarship: The Digital Dilemma" from *The Internet and the University: Forum 2002* that electronic journals – which are, in essence, rented by libraries instead of purchased like paper copies, first started this anxiety about preservation: "Publishers stopped selling journals to libraries. Instead, they licensed the electronic content to libraries...[t]he journal was no longer a well-defined entity, but rather a database that could be configured..." In addition, trends in libraries brought about a greater need (both internally created and externally applied) to bring in digital content that they licensed rather than owned. This produces fears on both sides of the digital library fence. On the one hand, institutions in general cannot afford the infrastructure to digitize their entire collections and at the same time support and sustain the scholarly output of its users (Marcum 2002).

10. See for example the initiatives put forth by the Digital Curation Centre (http://www.dcc.ac.uk/).

11. For a more detailed analysis of UVa's historical approach to sustaining digital scholarship see "How Do We Sustain Digital Scholarship?" (Daigle 2005).

12. In this particular sentiment, Marcum is paraphrasing Bernie Hurley from the University of California (Marcum 2002).

13. "Open access appears likely to better serve these new scholarly communication practices by facilitating text-mining; data and literature integration and interconnection; the construction of large-scale knowledge structures; the creation of co-laboratories that integrate the scholarly literature directly into knowledge creation and analysis environments; and the emergence of groups of scholars functioning as virtual organizations that casually cross institutional boundaries and thus are no longer served by the subscription-based access restrictions that are circumscribed by these organizational boundaries." (Lynch 2006).

REFERENCES CITED

ACLS. 2006. Our cultural commonwealth: The report of the American Council of Learned Societies Commission on Cyberinfrastructure for the Humanities and Social Sciences, ed. Marlo Welshons. http://www.acls.org/cyberinfrastructure/.

ARL. 2006. NSF and ARL conduct workshop on digital data stewardship. *ARL: A Bimonthly Report* 249: 4-5. http://www.arl.org/resources/pubs/br/br249.shtml.

Bement, Arden L. 2007. Cyberinfrastructure: The second revolution. *The Chronicle of Higher Education*, 53, no.18: January 5, B5-B6.

Brogan, Martha L. 2005. *A kaleidoscope of digital American literature*. Washington, D.C.: Digital Library Federation and Council on Library and Information Resources.

Chronicle. 2007. The library as search engine. *The Chronicle of Higher Education* 53, no. 18: January 5, B24.

Daigle, Bradley. 2005. How do we sustain digital scholarship? In *Free culture and the digital library: Symposium proceedings 2005*, ed. Martin Halbert, 230-402. Atlanta: MetaScholar Initiative.

Duderstadt, James L. and Luc E Weber. 2004. *Reinventing the research university.* London: Economica.

Lynch, Clifford A. 2003. Institutional repositories: Essential infrastructure for scholarship in the digital age. *ARL: A Bimonthly Report* 226: 1-7. http://www.arl.org/resources/pubs/br/br226/.

--. 2006. Improving access to research results: Six points. *ARL: A Bimonthly Report* 248: 5-7. http://www.arl.org/resources/pubs/br/br248.shtml.

Maloy, Frances. 2006. Scholarly communication – it is our problem! ARL/ACRL Institute on Scholarly Communication challenges, assumptions, and shifts perspectives. *ARL: A Bimonthly Report* 248: 8-10. http://www.arl.org/resources/pubs/br/br248.shtml.

Marcum, Deanna B. 2002. Preservation of scholarship: The digital dilemma." In *The internet and the university: Forum 2002*, ed. Maureen Devlin, 201-220. Boulder: Educause. http://www.educause.edu/forum/ffpiu02w.asp.

Modern Language Association. 2006. MLA task force on evaluating scholarship for tenure and promotion. http://www.mla.org/tenure_promotion.

Readings, Bill 1996. *The university in ruins.* Cambridge: Harvard University Press.

Schwartz, Candy 2000. Digital libraries: An overview. *The Journal of Academic Librarianship* 26, no. 6: 385-393.

Sustainability, Publishing, and Digital Libraries

Michael J. Furlough (Penn State University Libraries)

Abstract: Research libraries have begun experimenting with publishing services to intervene in the scholarly communications "crisis." These efforts have included direct support for publishing journals, the development of institutional repositories, collaborations with faculty to experiment with new forms of scholarship, and collaborations with university presses. Though the basis of many library publishing programs has been technology infrastructure, going forward these programs require focus on non-technological issues to ensure their sustainability. Just as traditional publishers do, libraries engaged in publishing will encounter economic challenges and must acknowledge the academic values that support the existing systems of publishing and which could inhibit the development of new ones. Collaborations with university presses suggest how libraries can address the needs of scholars and better understand publishing as a business and system. Though such collaborations are not free of business challenges and highlight potential conflicts arising from the traditional missions of each organization, they also offer the possibility of leveraging complementary skill sets to provide a strong basis for new publication services.

INTRODUCTION

The well-documented "crisis in scholarly communications," involving conglomeration in commercial publishing; extreme inflation in scientific, technical, and medical publishing (STM); decreasing purchasing power in libraries; and collateral damage in university press publishing has become a common topic in libraries and higher education in general.[1] The concept of "sustainability" has both economic and ecological connotations within conversations about scholarly communications, libraries, and publishing. These discussions have increasingly focused on the negative impact of publishing economics on what Bonnie Nardi and Vicky O'Day would refer to as the "information ecology" of the systems of publishing and acquisition that support scholarly communication (Nardi and O'Day 1999). But despite the last decade's economic pressures on libraries, we have also witnessed an enormous amount of research and development activity within digital library programs around the world. And librarians have begun to suggest and pioneer new roles for the library in the changing scholarly publishing environment, in part because the entrepreneurial nature of these programs has given librarians a different set of tools with which to intervene in this crisis.

A growing chorus of library leaders has argued that academia must "take control" back from the commercial publishers to realign scholarly communications with the academic mission. In response, libraries have begun to support scholarly publication more actively. In this essay, I will discuss sustainability through the lens of endeavors that range from services in collaboration with faculty on new forms of scholarship, to institutional repositories, to the deployment of these digital library platforms in support of journal and book publishing services. Libraries have pursued the latter both independently, and more recently, in collaboration with university presses. Kate Wittenberg writes that "librarians are trained to think particularly about user needs and services, and this focus may make it easier for them to use their skills in making decisions about what content to publish and in what format" (Wittenberg 2004). Publishers and librarians interact with research faculty in different capacities. While traditional publishers, unlike librarians, may not have a deep knowledge of their authors' needs as researchers, publishers (and some librarians) have also noted that it is crucial to understand and consider the needs of researchers as authors, and that librarians may not be well positioned in this respect. In a more recent blog posting, Peter Brantley starkly contradicted Wittenberg, arguing that librarians tend to have a flattened understanding of publishing, and concluding that "librarians are likely to be lousy publishers" because historically they have not worked with researchers as producers and authors, lack experience in cultivating new scholarly content, and have not mastered the systems of marketing necessary to ensure its uptake (Brantley 2007).

Much of the groundbreaking digital library work in the past decade has been funded heavily by grants and other research funds. Going forward, programs that undertake experimental digital library publishing activities must engage deeply with the issue of sustainability. The programs need to ensure that there will be adequate funding to support experiments as they become operational, and to generate new experiments to follow them. The consulting division of the Scholarly Publishing and Academic Resources Coalition, or SPARC, has pointed out that "no matter how innovative and compelling the concept, how important its mission, [a scholarly publishing initiative] must ultimately if not quickly become self-sustaining. That can best be achieved by project developers that adapt and apply sound business planning practices" (Goldstein 2002).[2] Libraries cannot become full-fledged business operations and revenue capture centers on their campuses, but the need for sustainability demands their attention to business activities with which libraries have historically had little experience.

Indeed, librarians' double-bind consists of their need to do more to forecast needs and trends for the emerging generation of scholars, while maintaining and even deepening existing services and systems on which today's (perhaps more conservative) scholars now depend. My discussion of scholarly publishing and digital libraries looks at both traditional and non-traditional scholarship, and focuses heavily, although not exclusively, on the humanities and social sciences and on emerging relationships between libraries and university press publishing. These are areas less frequently discussed than scientific, technical, and medical (STM) publication trends, but they have been affected heavily by those trends. The need for innovation and change within the system of scholarly communications dictates that new players, including digital libraries, can and should become outlets for publications of all sorts, including both peer-reviewed scholarship and less formal communications. In this essay I review both obstacles to and tactics for developing sustainable practices through a discussion of the field, and review some library-based publishing experiments that have yielded results toward developing sustainable business and service practices.

MISSIONS AND BUSINESS MODELS

As the business author Jim Collins has argued, successful not-for-profit organizations maximize their ability to support their institutional mission rather than investor profit (Collins 2005). For libraries, that mission can be distilled to supporting access to cultural and scholarly information in multiple formats, regardless of origin. Doing so requires systems and processes for collection, organization, stewardship, and preservation. Academic presses identify and acquire promising new books and journals, and consequently have elaborated processes of vetting; adding editorial, design, and production value; and investing in the marketing and dissemination of this new intellectual output. University presses, with varying levels of subsidy from their host institutions, originally developed to help support the publication of research that had little commercial value. While university library collections tend to reflect the breadth of their school's curriculum and their faculty's specializations, publishers cultivate a narrower focus on a few subject areas, building depth that enables them to compete with each other for high quality manuscripts. For a publisher, each title represents an investment of resources and the assumption of risk that the investment may not be returned. Successful publishing spreads risk across portfolios in an attempt to publish enough successful titles to cover the costs of others.

Economist Paul Courant, now the director of the University of Michigan Library, has frequently explained in economic terms that demand drives sustainability. For any activity, one must identify the value to potential users and find a way of having them (or their agents) pay to support it. Libraries are no exception to this rule, and they provide Courant with a useful example of this basic premise. Universities recognize the importance of having a research collection and related services available on campus, so they have become agents of the library user and have found ways of supporting the costs of managing such an enterprise. This imperfect funding model for "stitching together" resources over the longer-term has generally worked in favor of the libraries and the faculty and students they serve, though it does not address all factors as well as we might hope (Courant 2006b).[3] The library's basic business model entails receiving funds from the university, expending them on information resources and related services, and then providing these free of charge to the university's students, faculty, and staff.

Courant has also noted that the economics of "public goods," such as scholarship, are not generally bound by principles of scarcity, since ideas can be consumed without limiting another's ability to consume them. He points out, however, that this helps us with only one part of the business model to support scholarly communication:

> Unfortunately, although public goods can be extended to more users at zero cost, they can still be costly to produce in the first place. The case of digitally produced scholarship is of course an excellent example. What the theory tells us is that we ought to charge nothing for it at the margin – give it away. It tells nothing about how to pay for its production or how to determine how much to produce. What it tells us is that markets will under–produce (Courant 2006a).

Or these markets may overcharge and jealously protect ownership rights – as has arguably been occurring in some commercial academic publishing sectors. Because an existing public good costs little to re-use, a market based on distributing public goods must under-produce in order to extract capital from the market, or find alternative ways of generating revenue from those goods. Though university presses are supported to varying degrees by their host institutions, these not-for-profit publishers must also rely on the same academic publishing market as commercial publishers to (hopefully) raise enough money on some activities (such as journal publishing) to support publishing activities in a few areas that have limited sales appeal (such as humanities monographs).

Limited university support for academic publishing strengthens negative market forces that can inhibit scholarly communication. Every university has a library, but not all universities have academic presses, creating what has been called a "free-rider" effect. The American Association of University Presses counts only 107 full members affiliated with colleges and universities, while US doctoral and masters-granting institutions number nearly 1,000.[4] A limited number of institutions thus disproportionately bear the cost of academic publishing for the good of the entire academy. "University Publishing in a Digital Age," an important 2007 study from Ithaka, shows how university presses find themselves in a double-bind. They are one of the few units in a university expected to operate as a business and generate most of their own revenue. When they run a deficit, universities may float the difference, but "[n]ot surprisingly," the report states, "provosts put limited resources and attention towards what they perceive to be a service to the broader community....One provost confessed that 'the press has always been the next item on the list'" (Brown 2007). This imbalance heavily distorts the academic publishing market, and it has, according to the Ithaka report, ultimately contributed to the disconnection between presses and their host institutions, and to a lack of strategic thinking about publishing as a research infrastructure on campus. Struggling to manage their core operations, academic presses have had little capital, or inclination, to assume the additional investment costs and risks inherent in developing innovative publishing programs. Where academic publishers have done so, it has frequently been done with some substantial outside support, often from the same agencies to which libraries have turned for support of their digital projects, such as the Andrew W. Mellon Foundation.[5]

Librarians have limited experience with generating revenue – primarily through fees, including use fees to publishers and to other institutions for interlibrary loan – but these form a small part of what are generally very large budgets that can often more readily absorb new costs or experimental activities. Digitization services and digital library programs have brought added costs to library budgets, which have been paid for through funding from granting agencies, gifts, and occasional new money from the university, as well as a lot of clever re-allocation of existing funds and staff within libraries. In the short term, it seems that libraries can individually and collectively afford more risks in the technology arena than academic publishers. But engagement in publishing expands the library mission from supporting access (a more passive model) to include supporting dissemination (a more active model), and from spending revenue to finding ways of generating and capturing it. A library engaged in ongoing publishing activities will almost certainly confront the issues of revenue generation, cost recovery, and capital investment in an effort to create a sustainable program. In so doing, such libraries may find themselves moving away from the traditional business models of completely free access and services. Open access principles generally match a traditional library approach and are attractive distribution and access models in the eyes of many librarians. But the debate about open access business models centers on shifting the burden of subsidizing the cost of publishing away from consumers in the market to the producers (authors or publishers) or other agents acting on their behalf (libraries, provosts, or funding agencies). From an institutional perspective, library and university press budgets already provide the support for academic publishing. No subsidy now exists that could be moved between libraries and presses without incurring damage to one or both. No library can significantly curtail the buying and licensing (renting) of collections to instead shift funds to support its own publishing enterprise without incurring the wrath of local faculty.

Barring a substantial windfall from university administrators, sustainable publishing will thus require libraries and publishers to consider how to monetize services around scholarship without significantly inhibiting access. Obviously no library can compete with Elsevier directly as a publisher, but a library can work to meet needs that are not addressed well by large commercial publishers due to their scale. Library-based publishing should focus on the university press mission to support at-risk scholarship, but we must also keep in mind that this "at-risk" scholarship may prove financially challenging to support, and force consideration of how or if experimental publishing programs can more cost-effectively publish than a traditional one. Innovations are crucial, but in order to build upon them, library-based publishing will need to develop a business model responsive to an academic culture that is, in fact, often antithetical to radical innovations in scholarly communication methods.

ACADEMIC CULTURE AND SCHOLARLY COMMUNICATIONS

Beyond the communication of ideas, publishing plays a political and social role in establishing pathways for scholarly recognition and advancement. This provides a crucial context for business planning and experimental activities. While libraries and publishers have long recognized problems in the economic system of scholarly communications, it has been extraordinarily difficult to engage the attention of academic faculty and researchers whom they serve. Two reports published in 2006, one by the Modern Language Association and the other from the Center for Studies in Higher Education, attest to deeply embedded cultural resistance to certain types of change, outlining the author's perspective on academic publishing.

The Center for Studies in Higher Education at the University of California, Berkeley, reaffirmed the vital role of peer review and formal publication in establishing scholars' reputations and evaluating their work, even though significant questions exist about the quality and process of peer review. C. Judson King and Diane Harley titled their study "Scholarly Communication: Academic Values and Sustainable Models," and conducted in-depth interviews with senior faculty about their attitudes towards publishing and their own publishing practices. Interview subjects were drawn from Berkeley's departments of Anthropology, Biostatistics, Chemical Engineering, English, and Law and Economics. The most intriguing findings for libraries and publishers are the prospects for innovation and experimentation around the edges of traditional publishing that the study outlines in nearly all areas. Discussing their work in the *Journal of Electronic Publishing*, the authors suggest that a focus on the informal publishing activities of scholars can benefit the overall system, concluding that "innovations in in-progress communication will eventually drive improvements in final archival publication" (Harley 2007). Their work warns against attempts to move faculty away from peer-reviewed, archival publication, painting them as naïve and doomed to fail. In the humanities, use and communication patterns are most deeply rooted in the existing system. The authors found little knowledge of open access among the faculty members they surveyed and found open *skepticism* that "free" publications amounted to much more than vanity works. Thus the positive emphasis on informal publication channels must be considered in light of a discipline's dominant processes of authorship and culture of sharing. Across all disciplines, services supporting scholarly communication must consider what constitutes "in-progress" work, and what types of services and technologies will best serve researchers as authors.

The Modern Language Association's 2006 "Report on Evaluating Scholarship for Tenure and Promotion" confirms that professional advancement in the modern languages requires monograph publication in increasing volume:

> The status of the monograph as a gold standard is confirmed by the expectation in almost one-third of all departments surveyed (32.9%) of progress toward completion of a second book for tenure. This expectation is even higher in doctorate-granting institutions, where 49.8% of departments now demand progress toward a second book. (MLA 2006)

Though the report broadly calls for decreasing emphasis on monographic publication, its survey of department heads reports a large degree of acceptance for the current state of affairs even while many departments are reviewing their processes and expectations. The MLA argues strongly through this report that the promotion and tenure system relies too heavily on forms of economically threatened publishing. Yet because scholars have limited understanding of publishing's broader contexts, the report provides only the starting point for what would be a very long road to reform. For example, though many modern language journals appear online through aggregators such as Project Muse, the MLA reports that "40.8% of departments in doctorate granting institutions report no experience evaluating refereed articles in electronic format, and 65.7% report no experience evaluating monographs in electronic format" (MLA 2006). Though both publishers and libraries have a significant stake in promoting reforms to this state of affairs, these must be based in the disciplines themselves; librarians and publishers may work together to advise on these matters, but they do not have the credibility to lead or instigate them.

These two reports depict a strong status quo, but provide glimmers of hope for change. In general, the humanities do not have a strong culture of sharing work-in-progress except in conferences and symposia, which usually do not have published proceedings. Academic blogs in the humanities, where papers and presentations are often workshopped by commentators, offer interesting examples contradicting this trend.[6] Furthermore, the peer-review methods emerging in decentralized information environments such as social networking systems and even e-commerce sites suggest some possible ways in which scholarly authority could be conferred in addition to peer-review (Wittenberg 2007; Jensen 2007). Nevertheless, academic culture replicates itself powerfully. Any publishing program established with the aim of promulgating change will still have to acknowledge commitments to the existing system in addition to any experimental reforms it may wish to propose. The Center for Studies in Higher Education report reminds us that the specific forms of communications vary by discipline, producing multiple coexistent scholarly communication systems. The MLA report, though written to provoke change, suggests how very deeply rooted specific forms of communication are within the humanities. Library-based publishing in the humanities might thus focus on finding better ways to author, publish, and distribute monographic literature. More challenging and difficult to support, however, are services and programs to enable digital scholarship that re-shapes what the scholarly monographic argument might look like.

COLLABORATIVE E-MONOGRAPH PUBLISHING

Experiments with business models and delivery systems for monograph publishing and online delivery have the potential to impact how university presses achieve their mission. Monographs are firmly entrenched in the humanities even though the economic system that enabled a press to rely on many hundreds of library purchases no longer exists. While users have been hesitant to adopt book-length materials online over the past few years, recently there have been signs of greater acceptance, and it seems clear that cover-to-cover reading is only one aspect of research. We are now starting to see collaborations between presses and libraries that address the business and access models for electronic monograph delivery, while still acknowledging reader preferences for print. These collaborations also show potential areas of conflict among missions and business models of presses and libraries.

The California Digital Library's eScholarship Editions provide an interesting example of the intersection between publishing and library collection building activities, illustrating the technology oriented tradeoffs librarians may face when developing such partnerships. The California Digital Library (CDL) began partnering with the University of California Press (UCP) in 2003 to produce the eScholarship Editions collection. In essence, this was a collection development project to underwrite continued access for UC users by funding a major part of the conversion of previously published UCP books. UC librarians initiated the project by using collection development funds to buy copies of the electronic source versions of all monographs that UCP had licensed to NetLibrary as that business threatened to fail and thereby end electronic access to that material. Roughly 2,000 of NetLibrary's files, XHMTL-encoded UCP books, were further processed by CDL technical staff to bring them into conformance to CDL's own internal standards for XML-encoded full-text objects, enabling their delivery via the CDL digital library infrastructure. According to Catherine Candee, director of eScholarship Services in the California Digital Library, the projected cost of extending this full XML conversion to more backlist titles not previously digitized was high enough to make them reconsider their options and plans. Once converted, such data are portable and exportable to other formats, but few users seem to take direct advantage of the XML encoding in search and delivery online. While for highly specialized texts, such as the scholarly editions of Mark Twain now underway at UCP, full-text XML markup is of course crucial, CDL's experiment requires a consideration of the threshold of "good enough" for converting monographic reprints. Candee explains that future collaborations between CDL and UCP for monograph publishing will focus on publishing directly to online services (Candee 2007).

In late 2006, the University of California Press announced a call for manuscripts for Flashpoints, a new series intended to be delivered online freely and for sale in print. Similarly, in early 2007, the Scholarly Publishing Office and University of Michigan Press released its first title in a new collaboratively published series, called digitalculturebooks, making it entirely available online for free and for sale in print. Late in 2007, the Office of Digital Scholarly Publishing, a collaborative venture between the Penn State Press and Penn State University Libraries, released three new titles in a revived series, Penn State Romance Studies.[7] Flashpoints and digitalculturebooks are new series that are aimed at new markets, but Penn State Romance Studies attempts to use electronic publishing and printing technology to revive a previously existing series of monographs. Penn State Romance Studies publishes literary and cultural studies in French, Italian, Spanish and Portuguese subjects. Originally begun in the early

1990s as a traditional monograph series in literary criticism, it was cancelled later, when, owing partly to financial pressures, the Penn State Press curtailed publishing in literary criticism. Its revival in collaboration with the Libraries was not based on a change in the market for the scholarship, but was rather a joint decision to focus on support to under-served areas. Like Flashpoints and digitalculturebooks, Romance Studies intends to take advantage of less expensive print-on-demand technology for short run printing. However, the cost of acquisition, editorial review, and production are largely the same for an e-monograph as for a traditional monograph, and outweigh the costs of inventory management and printing in the overall cost of book publishing.

The business and access models for these series take a cue from the National Academy Press's earlier experiments, in which Academy publications that were offered online for free viewing apparently resulted in increased hard-copy sales (Pope 1999). Penn State expects that libraries will continue to acquire the Romance Studies titles in print through approval plans, and hopes that individual sales will be higher because of the accessibility of the content online. For publishers, "free content online" raises a significant question about how to promote usage without cannibalizing sales. In the case of both digitalculturebooks and Romance Studies, titles can be read in their entirety online by accessing individual chapters or paging through the book, but in neither case can you obtain the entire book with a single click.[8] In these models, on-demand printing and binding represent fee-based services around free content, providing online readers with a hard-copy access that they may prefer to reading on screen. Betting on eye-strain is obviously not a long-term business strategy, however. An e-monograph's benchmarks for success should include increased readership and citations and improved utility, not only increased sales for a "real" print publication. These three experiments should mark the first steps towards injecting mainstream contemporary scholarly content into a user-focused system of digital library services and collections that could change how monographs are published and used, and how they interact with related monographs, journals, and supporting evidence available elsewhere online. Publishing digital content requires its entrance into a multi-node network of discovery and use that only just begins when preparing it for web viewing.

The need for scale and aggregation are further considerations for the sustainability of these monograph experiments. For online readers, smaller piles of content are less attractive and useful than larger piles, while for producers, small projects are less efficient and must compete for attention and resources. Developing strategies to incorporate e-monographs such as these into larger aggregations (preferably subject- and discipline-, rather than producer-based) would contribute to the viability of e-monograph publishing programs. The previously mentioned Ithaka report on university publishing argues strongly for a "shared electronic publishing infrastructure across universities" in order to "save costs, create scale, leverage expertise, innovate, unite the resources of the university (e.g. libraries, presses, faculty, student body, IT), extend the brand of American higher education (and each particular university within that brand), create a blended interlinked environment of fee-based to free information, and provide a robust alternative to commercial competitors" (Brown 2007). While it is hard to argue with this huge list of desired outcomes, it could certainly be read as a suggestion that small efforts have a limited future, or none at all. But in spite of this emphasis on the need for scale, the report encourages collaborations on e-publishing such as those at California, Michigan, and Penn State. I would argue that experiments with e-monographs should be strategically undertaken as steps towards developing such a system collaboratively, rather than simply ceding this responsibility to third parties.

DIGITAL SCHOLARSHIP IN THE HUMANITIES

Digital scholarship in the humanities has demonstrated modes of extended argument and interpretive exploration that move away from the monograph form, suggesting a novel future in the field. The pace of this work accelerated over the past twenty years as it became deeply entwined with digital library research in academic libraries, but it continues to pose special technological challenges. At its best, such work takes advantage of the medium to develop truly new modes of inquiry, presented through forms of argument, evidence, and analysis that would not be possible without information technology. Some of the best known examples include two pioneering projects: the Valley of the Shadow, led by Ed Ayers and Will Thomas, and the Rossetti Archive, led by Jerome McGann, the first two of many rich, intricate scholarly editing and compilation projects sponsored by the Institute for Advanced Technology in the Humanities (IATH) at the University of Virginia.[9] The prize-winning dissertations that are being redeveloped into electronic monographs through Gutenberg-E at the Electronic Publishing Initiative at Columbia (EPIC) have emerged as another highly visible set of experiments in this area.[10] As we might expect, for scholars themselves, having such work recognized by peers may be particularly challenging. Because of the nature of such work, it has often developed outside of the normal publication process that brings peer review, and has rarely been led by junior scholars. The MLA report, discussed above, attests to the limited experience faculty have in evaluating traditional forms of scholarship in digital format, much less non-standard scholarly forms (MLA 2006). Even when reviewed by peers, work substantially deviating from expected generic forms may proceed through a bumpy review process.[11]

Such works are also difficult, time consuming, and costly to produce. For publishers, librarians, and technologists, they pose significant challenges for standardization and management. Supporting Digital Scholarship (SDS), a grant by the Andrew W. Mellon Foundation to IATH and the University of Virginia Library, conducted a broad investigation of the issues involved in developing and sustaining such projects. Monographs and journal articles are fairly predictable genres, and libraries have well-established methods for storing and preserving them (at least in print). Digital humanities scholarship has spawned unstable genres that have resisted standardization in the name of innovation. Humanities work tends towards idiosyncrasy, and scholars may argue both that their topic and mode of exploration demand specific technological approaches.[12] But what does it mean to "collect," much less "publish" complex archives of multi-media for which scholars have developed their own standards of markup, metadata authorities, and user interfaces, but which also makes significant use of commercially produced software that will one day cease to be supported by its maker? Significant variation will lead to approaches that do not scale technologically or economically, and the SDS reports openly contemplate the likelihood that many forms of presentation and evidence may not be able to be preserved (Unsworth 2000). For libraries and publishers, long-term dissemination of these efforts requires collaboration in their development from the very start in order to build resources using methods that can be sustained long-term.

Digital humanities work requires collaboration more than most humanities work, contrasting with the traditional model of the solitary scholar-monk in the cell, stacks, or carrel. Library staff supporting these scholars may find themselves in an unfamiliar role of content developers, closer to editors than traditional librarians. The challenges require substantial investments in the humanities and social sciences and significant changes in the way we support the development of scholarship, as recent studies have argued (ACLS 2006). Moving beyond the experimental stages in this area will be difficult given the limited (and limiting) institutional support for such activity and the correspondingly slow uptake among the current generation of scholars. Digital humanities scholarship exemplifies the conundrum for libraries in developing sustainable, yet innovative support for both mature and fledgling systems of scholarly communication.

THE ROLE OF INSTITUTIONAL REPOSITORIES

Few libraries have undertaken collaborative digital humanities projects, but more have focused on developing scalable infrastructure to support digital archiving of more traditional types of scholarship and related library collections. The institutional repository movement, which emerged over the past decade, is rhetorically linked both to traditional library missions (archiving university materials, providing service to the institution, promoting openness in access to information) and alarming library pressures (increased journal costs, dwindling public support for higher education, recessions). The link to traditional missions is strong and obvious. In contrast, the link to the promise of decreasing journal costs is largely theoretical at this point. Excepting Google's various activities, institutional repositories (IRs) have probably had more impact within research library circles over the past decade than any other digital library development. A 2005 Coalition for Networked Information survey concluded that they are "now clearly and broadly being recognized as essential infrastructure for scholarship in the digital world" (Lynch 2005). This statement refers to recognitions by librarians and by administrators. The impact of IRs upon researchers has been less impressive and more uneven, and many repository services have struggled to engage faculty to ensure deposit of their work.

As Nancy Fried Foster and Susan Gibbons have pointed out, the value of a repository containing the total research output of an institution may be hard to convey to individual researchers. A faculty member must see the IR's potential utility for and impact on his or her scholarship and academic stature (Foster 2005).[13] IRs may support publication-related activities, and may provide a platform from which journals, proceedings, and other works can be "published," but they are not generally seen by faculty as a substitute for brand-name publication outlets, nor will they be as they are currently deployed. The unifying theme of an "institutional repository" is, after all the *institution*, not the disciplines in which researchers validate their scholarly identities. Researchers, not librarians and publishers, determine the value of an academic publication and highly valued journals tend to focus exclusively on particular domains. "Each discipline has a normative culture, largely defined by their reward system and traditions," write Phillip Davis and Matthew Connolly in a case study of Cornell University's institutional repository. "If the goal of institutional repositories is to capture and preserve the scholarship of one's faculty, institutional repositories will need to address this cultural diversity" (Davis 2007). In contrast, a disciplinary-based repository of pre- and post-prints can become a valued resource in a given community that relies upon sharing works-in-progress, as the arXiv service, based now at Cornell University Library, has shown for Physics.[14] The arXiv also shows that an open-access repository can play a large role in establishing research priority and validity, without supplanting the core canonical publication outlets.

Library programs that can support a disciplinary-based repository, either in addition to or instead of institutionally-based services, may have an edge in developing a service with value to researchers that could influence future publication models. Such collections should not be confined to textually based gray literature, but could include ancillary materials in many formats and genres. Data-driven fields in the sciences and social sciences are promising areas for the development of publication-related archiving through institutional repositories. Publishers have so far shown limited ability to distribute or combine original research datasets with articles or technical reports that are based on those data. Meanwhile, funding agencies are increasingly focused on the continued archiving of data produced during the course of research. Joe Esposito makes a similar point in a recent essay, but argues for greater involvement from university presses, which, he believes "would immediately see that the output of a single institution would make for thin gruel and would impose on the repository the discipline and practices of a publisher: What fields are ripe for repositories? Who are the key authors in the field, and how do we attract them to participate?" (Esposito 2007). Esposito somewhat misses the point that IRs do have a valid archiving role to play, but his remarks suggest a potentially interesting avenue of collaboration between libraries and presses in the elaboration of repository services, one where publishing and preservation models could potentially meet. He also notes that no press has the funding to invest in this activity. But libraries have already invested, and they have often done so without successful plans for marketing both the service and the content, and with limited interest in how such a service could be monetized to help sustain it. The development of a robust system to support the life cycle of authorship, sharing, and archiving, that would co-exist with existing publication channels, could be a promising area for collaborative research and experimentation between libraries and publishers.

LIBRARIES AS PUBLISHING SERVICE PROVIDERS

Information technology deployments within libraries ground all library-based publishing experiments. Digital humanities work and institutional repositories are two areas where digital library services have been deployed to focus on emerging activities, but there are still significant traditional publishing-related services in which digital library programs have played a role, as we have seen with e-monograph experiments. Journal publishing is somewhat different. Compared to book publishing, where a publisher must invest in editorial and acquisitions staff to identify promising authors and their manuscripts, much of the content development for journals takes place among editorial boards external to a publisher. Libraries with a significant commitment to developing technology infrastructure can sometimes leverage these investments to act as a web-hosting service or even as a full-fledged publisher, working directly with authors and editorial boards, rather than publishers, to provide the ability to publish electronically. There are some significant and well established library-based publishing services in this arena.

The University of Michigan Scholarly Publishing Office (SPO), for example, provides client-based services that build upon Michigan's well-developed digital library infrastructure that manages a large online collection of reformatted texts. Since the mid-1990s Michigan's Digital Library Production Services has developed both a well-regarded set of services for large-scale text digitization, and the DLXS software for management of digital assets on a significant scale. The University of Michigan Library's digital collections – exclusive of the titles scanned in partnership with Google – number in the tens of thousands of items. The Scholarly Publishing Office leverages this activity to offer scholarly societies or other publishing clients the services of digitization, production, hosting, and even print services outsourced through Lightning Source and Amazon BookSurge. The principles of selection for their digitized library collections and the principles of client selection within the SPO serve different business goals, and these activities remain separate cost centers within the library. The venture relies on a mixed business model to support its activities, aligning them with a focus on limiting barriers to access to scholarship. The office includes a staff of six, with three staff supported entirely by revenue-generating activities. As of February 2007, SPO served as the online host of 15 journals, with a few more in development. SPO also serves as the hosting agent for the ACLS History E-Book project and the Law Library Microform Consortium, its two largest clients. According to director Maria Bonn, SPO assesses fees for its services to revenue generating and subscription based projects to offset the costs of the publications of smaller organizations and to encourage them to provide their publications in an open-access model (Bonn 2007).

Project Euclid, based at Cornell University Library, provides non-profit publishing services for 50 journals in mathematics and statistics. The subject-oriented focus for Euclid enables staff to develop specialized support for a community requiring specific character sets and markup languages, linkages to the premier literature databases (Math Reviews and Zentrallblatt MATH), as well as a deeper understanding of the market for the content. It has also allowed Euclid to develop as a brand in itself, enabling it to both draw new clients and sell access to existing ones. Unlike SPO, whose clients, such as the ACLS E-book Project, market their own work, Cornell University Library has assumed responsibility for marketing, subscription management, and order fulfillment for some titles available from Euclid. Like SPO, its portfolio includes a mix of access models, working to support open access as much as possible. Terry Ehling, director of the Center for Innovative Publishing at Cornell University Library, explains that running such a publishing service inside a library presents significant financial and cultural challenges, especially when it begins as a start up. "While Euclid has achieved a measure of financial and operational stability, and has realized cost-sustainability," Ehling relates, "it is essentially a small business (a revenue-capture unit) operating inside a library (a cost center)." Euclid requires a number of business operations, including marketing and back office management, for which libraries typically do not have deep expertise, but which must be developed or outsourced for a sustainable and credible operation (Ehling 2007).

These developing programs' year-to-year stability requires income to support ongoing maintenance and new technological developments expected by their clients and readers. A digital library program's asset management services, such as Michigan's DLXS, can be used to support publishing activities. But Bonn acknowledges that overall the system was designed for broader use cases of digital asset management, and that SPO sometimes requires additional work in preparing and managing serial content for the delivery specified by clients (Bonn 2007). Euclid's technology platform was developed with support from the Andrew W. Mellon Foundation specifically to support publication services of serial content, not digital library content management in the broad sense. In 2004, Cornell University Library and Penn State University Libraries received further support from the Mellon Foundation to generalize the Euclid software to a new, open source version known as DPubS, which supports journals, conference proceedings, monographs, and potentially other publishing formats.[15] DPubS, as well as the Public Knowledge Project's Open Journal Systems software, are both intended to provide academic libraries and even individuals with low-cost tools to support publishing activities independent of larger digital asset management infrastructures.[16] The existence of such tools assumes a significant need to make more widespread the use of technology to support publication throughout various sectors of the academy, not just libraries and publishers. But it remains to be seen whether the potential community of users of such software – which could include libraries, publishers and academic departments – is large enough to sustain the ongoing development and maintenance of code needed to give tools such as these a viable life beyond their originating institutions.

CONCLUSION: TECHNOLOGY, COLLABORATION, AND SUSTAINABILITY

As a subset of digital library activities, publishing services inherit many of the same sustainability issues, including evolving (and competing) standards and the fragility of digital preservation methods. Libraries' large scale infrastructure investments threaten to become liabilities without effective management and continued reinvestment to keep systems robust, and where necessary, to keep up with the commercial sector and its large scale capital investments. Arguably, some of the most innovative digital publishing occurs within the more lucrative STM fields, where large for-profits have significant capital to invest in systems supporting citation analysis and linking, reader reviews, tagging, annotation, and personal collection-building. In this decade, libraries have begun to shift emphasis to large-scale collaborations and interoperability efforts, such as the Digital Library Federation (DLF) Aquifer initiative, and the positioning of "hosted solution" services. Both could de-emphasize the importance of local library content management, which has been the basis of most publishing experiments. It will be important to watch how libraries and publishers invest in technology in the next five years, how the market for outsourced software and services affect those investments, and how both affect publishing channels.

However, if libraries and publishers are to continue collaborating, and if they have any hope of developing innovative and sustainable publishing services together, such collaborations will have to be based on more than the provision of technology services. These efforts should result in not just "understanding" in the abstract sense, but also in hybridized activities that will influence the decisions of either organization going forward. Such collaborations could focus on determining the threshold of economic sustainability for various types of activities, and they should address the ecology of scholarly communications practices in addition to its economics. The simplified version of the library mission defines it as "supporting access," and a simplified version of the academic press's mission defines it as "supporting creation and dissemination." We see online how these dissemination activities of presses and access activities of libraries blur and overlap. But dissemination and providing access are not the same as publishing. What can be lost in the blurring are the multi-faceted business operations and choices that stand behind content selection, cultivation, dissemination and access. Collaborations may help to clarify these activities for all players involved.

The Romance Studies series of the Office of Digital Scholarly Publishing (ODSP) resulted from several years of small experiments between the Penn State University Libraries and Penn State Press, all aimed at building trust and at uncovering what each organization could learn from the other (Eaton 2004). Not just the series, but also the organizational structure that supports its publication is currently an experiment. The Press, though now administratively a part of the libraries, remains a separately funded budget center with its own operating funds and staff. The ODSP serves as the site of collaboration between the Press and the Libraries, operated jointly by two co-directors drawn from senior management in both. As a start up, staffing to the ODSP comes from existing staff and service departments in both organizations to form product project teams. The distributed nature serves an important aim, however, in that it enables staff and administrators to cross organizational lines and gain a better understanding of each group's mission and business operations. But distributed activities in both the Library and the Press also create administrative challenges, including ensuring the smooth flow of information, accurately capturing internal costs to support pricing any fee-based services, and aligning existing library technology and production services to support a cost-recovery venture. Like other innovative publishing services at Michigan, California, and Cornell, ODSP is trying to identify business models that will best support scholarly communications in low-cost areas that are otherwise threatened and assist in the development of communications channels in emerging areas.

A library involved in publishing is linked more closely to its local researchers than most publishers, and has an opportunity to tie the output of scholarship to real needs for forms of access, discovery, delivery, and use in their campus classrooms and labs. If demand drives sustainability, as Courant argues, a sustainable organization's mission will be oriented towards finding and addressing unmet needs. Such needs are sometimes more evolutionary than revolutionary, and may yield results that initially seem rather less interesting in comparison to what we can imagine as possible. In conservative academic cultures we must also recognize the potentially limited role that experiments and digital library research play in changing the nature of the scholarly communication systems, and partner directly with researchers to create models that will serve them best. Innovation still must be undertaken to move academics forward in their understanding of how changes in publication methods and scholarship do not conflict with standards of peer-review and archival publication. Sustainable digital publishing – ultimately a socially-bound and technologically-bound challenge – requires continued investment in collaborative activities across organizational lines to elaborate models of support.

ACKNOWLEDGEMENTS

I am indebted to Patrick Alexander, Maria Bonn, Terry Ehling, Eleanor Goodman, Katherine Skinner, Jack Sulzer, and Sandy

Thatcher, all of whom made this a better essay by generously providing comments on various drafts.

NOTES

1. The commentary on this topic is extensive, and has now ranged over four decades. The rise of electronic publishing in the early 1990s gave the topic new urgency. For a sample of the historical record, see Andrew Cummings, et. al., "University Libraries and Scholarly Communication: A study prepared for the Andrew W. Mellon Foundation"; Sanford G. Thatcher, "The Crisis in Scholarly Communication"; and the proceedings of the conference "The Specialized Scholarly Monograph in Crisis: Or How Can I Get Tenure If You Won't Publish My Book?" The latter includes a paper by Thatcher that reviews the literature on this topic back to the early 1970s (Cummings 1992; Thatcher 1995, 1997).
2. SPARC: http://www.arl.org/sparc/.
3. Thanks to Paul Courant for making the notes for this presentation available to me for review.
4. The 2005 Carnegie classifications include 282 research and doctoral granting universities and another 665 master's colleges and universities (Carnegie Foundation 2006). The full AAUP membership is 128, but not all members are directly affiliated with a university. Only 66 of these presses are located at a university where the library is a member of the Association of Research Libraries.
5. Project Muse began as a collaborative effort between the Johns Hopkins University Press and the Milton S. Eisenhower Library with funding from the National Endowment for the Humanities and the Andrew W. Mellon Foundation (http://muse.jhu.edu/). The University of Virginia Press also launched its Electronic Imprint with substantial investments from the Mellon Foundation. The goal of the Electronic Imprint has been to provide a publication outlet for digital scholarship in the humanities; this is an especially risky venture owing to the emerging and unstable nature of that particular field, as I will show later (http://www.ei.virginia.edu/).
6. See, for instance, *The Valve*, a blog sponsored by the Association of Literary Critics and Scholars that positions itself as an electronic "little magazine." Roughly a dozen authors post on a variety of topics in literary and cultural criticism, and frequently include drafts of essays or presentations for comment. *The Valve* has also sponsored engagement with new scholarship through "book events," which are essentially book reviews coordinated across multiple academic blogs over a given time span (http://www.thevalve.org/).
7. Flashpoints: http://www.ucpress.edu/books/UCFLA.ser.html; digitalculturebooks: http://www.digitalculture.org/; Penn State Romance Studies: http://romancestudies.psu.edu.

8. At least as of August 2007. As I am trying to suggest here, the decision-making in these new experiments is still quite fluid.
9. The Valley of the Shadow: http://valley.vcdh.virginia.edu/; The Rossetti Archive: http://www.rossettiarchive.org/; Institute for Advanced Technology in the Humanities: http://www.iath.virginia.edu/.
10. Gutenberg-E: http://www.gutenberg-e.org/; EPIC: http://www.epic.columbia.edu/.
11. When Ayers and Thomas presented an electronic article to the editors of the *American Historical Review*, they had to substantially revise it to match editors' expectations for the explication of historical analysis in a journal article (Ayers 2004). Others have attempted to develop mechanisms for review of such scholarship on its own merits. NINES (Networked Infrastructure for Nineteenth-Century Electronic Scholarship), a scholarly collective led by Jerome McGann, has set out to "establish an integrated publishing environment for aggregated, peer-reviewed online scholarship centered in nineteenth-century studies, British and American" (http://www.nines.org). The Electronic Imprint at the University of Virginia Press and the Gutenberg-E project at EPIC both aim to provide a peer-review and publication process for such scholarship.
12. Compare the approach of two products from the University of Virginia Press's Electronic Imprint, Clotel: *an Electronic Scholarly Edition* and *Herman Melville's* "Typee:" *A Fluid Text Edition*. Though both publications illuminate textual changes among multiple instantiations of their subject texts, they rely on different forms of programming, XML markup, and user interfaces (Brown 2006; Melville 2006).
13. In a more recent essay, these authors, along with others, also suggest that conservative cultural norms in academic libraries can also hamper the development of successful programs around institutional repositories and other innovative services (Foster 2007).
14. arXiv: http://arxiv.org.
15. DPubS: http://dpubs.org.
16. The Public Knowledge Project, jointly hosted at Simon Fraser University and the University of British Columbia, has been led by John Willinsky (now at Stanford University), and serves as a multifaceted exploration of how technology increases the value of scholarship for researchers and the public, Open Journal Systems has been quite successful in providing small organizations with a means of publishing scholarly journals online in both open-access and subscription forms. http://pkp.sfu.ca/.

REFERENCES CITED

ACLS. 2006. *Our cultural commonwealth: The report of the American Council of Learned Societies Commission on Cyberinfrastructure for the Humanities and Social Sciences*, ed. Marlo Welshons. http://www.acls.org/cyberinfrastructure/.

Ayers, Edward L. 2004. The academic culture and the IT culture: Their effect on teaching and scholarship. *EDUCAUSE Review* 39, no. 6, http://www.educause.edu/apps/er/erm04/erm0462.asp (accessed August 18, 2007).

Bonn, Maria. 2007. Phone conversation between Maria Bonn and Michael Furlough, February 1, 2007.

Brantley, Peter. 2007. Peter Brantley's thoughts and speculations: On scholarly communication and university presses, June 8, 2007. http://blogs.lib.berkeley.edu/shimenawa.php/2007/06/08/on_scholarly_communication_and_universit (accessed August 18, 2007).

Brown, Laura, Rebecca Griffiths, and Matthew Rascoff. 2007. *University publishing in a digital age*. New York. Ithaka. http://www.ithaka.org/strategic-services/university-publishing (accessed August 13, 2007).

Brown, William Wells. 2006. *Clotel: An electronic scholarly edition*, ed. C. Mulvey. Charlottesville: University of Virginia Press. http://rotunda.upress.virginia.edu:8080/clotel/ (accessed August 17, 2007).

Candee, Catherine. 2007. Phone conversation between Catherine Candee and Michael Furlough, January 18, 2007.

Carnegie Foundation, The. 2006. *Basic classification: Distribution of institutions and enrollments by classification category*. The Carnegie Foundation for the Advancement of Teaching. http://www.carnegiefoundation.org/classifications/index.asp?key=805 (accessed August 16, 2007).

Collins, Jim. 2005. *Good to great and the social sectors: Why business thinking is not the answer*. Boulder, CO: Jim Collins.

Courant, Paul N. 2006a. Scholarship and academic libraries (and their kin) in the world of Google. *First Monday* 11, no. 8, http://firstmonday.org/issues/issue11_8/courant/index.html (accessed January 27, 2007).

— — —. 2006b. Thoughts on economics and sustainability of things digital. Conference paper presented at the Sustaining Digital Libraries Symposium, October 4, 2006, at Emory University in Atlanta, GA.

Cummings, Andrew M., Marcia L. Witt, William G. Bowen, Laura O. Lazarus, and Richard H. Ekman. 1992. *University libraries and scholarly communication: A study prepared for the Andrew W. Mellon Foundation*. Washington, DC: Association of Research

Libraries. http://etext.virginia.edu/subjects/mellon/index.html (accessed August 15, 2007).

Davis, Phillip M., and Matthew J. L. Connolly. 2007. Institutional repositories: Evaluating the reasons for non-use of Cornell University's installation of DSpace. *D-Lib Magazine* 13, no. 3/4, http://www.dlib.org/dlib/march07/davis/03davis.html (accessed August 13, 2007).

Eaton, Nancy, Bonnie MacEwan, and Peter J. Potter. 2004. Learning to work together: The libraries and the University Press at Penn State. *Journal of Scholarly Publishing* 35, no. 4:215-220.

Ehling, Terry. 2007. Personal conversation between Terry Ehling and Michael Furlough. Seattle, WA, January 22, 2007.

Esposito, Joseph J. 2007. The wisdom of Oz: The role of the university press in scholarly communications. *Journal of Electronic Publishing* 10, no. 1, http://hdl.handle.net/2027/spo.3336451.0010.103 (accessed August 18, 2007).

Foster, Nancy Fried, and Susan Gibbons. 2005. Understanding faculty to improve content recruitment for institutional repositories. *D-Lib Magazine* 11, no. 1, http://www.dlib.org/dlib/january05/foster/01foster.html (accessed August 18, 2007).

Foster, Nancy Fried, Susan Gibbons, Suzanne Bell, and David Lindahl. 2007. *Institutional repositories, policies, and disruption.* Rochester: University of Rochester. http://hdl.handle.net/1802/3865. (accessed August 12, 2007).

Goldstein, Howard. 2002. *Gaining independence: A manual for planning the launch of a nonprofit electronic publishing venture.* Washington, DC: Scholarly Publishing and Academic Resources Coalition. http://www.arl.org/sparc/GI/ (accessed August 18, 2007).

Harley, Diane, Sarah Earl-Novell, Jennifer Arter, Shannon Lawrence, and C. Judson King. 2007. The influence of academic values on scholarly publication and communication practices. *Journal of Electronic Publishing* 10, no. 2, http://hdl.handle.net/2027/spo.3336451.0010.204 (accessed August 18, 2007).

Jensen, Michael. 2007. The new metrics of scholarly authority. *The Chronicle of Higher Education*, June 15, 2007, B6.

Lynch, Clifford and Joan Lippincott. 2005. Institutional repository deployment in the United States as of early 2005. *D-Lib Magazine* 11, no.9, http://www.dlib.org/dlib/september05/lynch/09lynch.html (accessed August 18, 2007).

Melville, Herman. 2006. *Herman Melville's "Typee:" A fluid text edition*, ed. J. Bryant. Charlottesville: University of Virginia Press. http://rotunda.upress.virginia.edu/Melville/ (accessed August 17, 2007).

MLA. 2006. *Modern Language Association Task Force on evaluating scholarship for tenure and promotion*. New York: Modern Language Association. http://www.mla.org/tenure_promotion (accessed August 18, 2007).

Nardi, Bonnie A., and Vicky L. O'Day. 1999. *Information ecologies: Using technology with heart*. Cambridge: The MIT Press.

Pope, Barbara Klein. 1999. National Academy Press: A case study. *Journal of Electronic Publishing* 4, no. 4, http://www.press.umich.edu/jep/04-04/pope.html (accessed August 18, 2007).

Thatcher, Sandford G. 1995. The crisis in scholarly communication. *The Chronicle of Higher Education*, March 3, 1995, B1-B2.

– – –. 1997. Thinking systematically about the crisis in scholarly communication. Paper presented at The Specialized Scholarly Monograph in Crisis: Or How Can I Get Tenure If You Won't Publish My Book?, September 11-12, in Washington, D.C.

Unsworth, John, and Thornton Staples. 2000. Supporting digital scholarship project. Institute for Advanced Technology in the Humanities and University Libraries, University of Virginia, Charlottesville, VA.2000-2003. Andrew W. Mellon Foundation. http://www3.iath.virginia.edu/sds/ (accessed August 18, 2007).

Wittenberg, Kate. 2004. Librarians as publishers: A new role in scholarly communication. *Searcher* 12, no. 10:50-53.

– – –. 2007. Credibility of content and the future of research, learning, and publishing in the digital environment. *Journal of Electronic Publishing* 10, no. 1, http://hdl.handle.net/2027/spo.3336451.0010.101 (accessed August 18, 2007).

Principles and Activities of Digital Curation for Developing Successful and Sustainable Repositories

Leslie Johnston (University of Virginia)

Abstract: As the development of Digital Library repositories has progressed, the definition of local digital curation principles has evolved to encompass not only intellectual curation, but also issues of standards and preservation that are enforced through best practices and systems architecture. Digital curation is the creation of a collection that supports a community's teaching and research, a collection that is managed and preserved not just for their current use but for future scholarly uses and technologies that we have not yet even imagined. This article covers four overarching principles of digital curation: Principles for Selection, Principles for the Use of Standards, Principles for Trustworthiness, and Principles for Preservation and Sustainability. These principles provide a model for organizations to identify goals for the creation of an architecture with which to create a trusted, managed repository environment, discovery and delivery services, and tools for the use of objects.

REPOSITORY DEVELOPMENT AT UVA

In 2002, the University of Virginia (UVa) Library began working toward the development of a Digital Collections Repository on top of Fedora™ (Johnston, 2005). Fedora – Flexible, Extensible Digital Object Repository Architecture – is a generalized digital asset management (DAM) architecture, upon which many types of digital library systems can be built (Lagoze, Payette, Shin, Wilper, 2006).[1] When we began the project, we were thinking about curation in the most traditional sense of the word – that digital collections would be evaluated and selected using the same subject-based criteria and expertise as the physical collections. At the time, curation of collections seemed a different effort than the stewardship of the digital objects.

As our work has progressed toward the development and launch of a Digital Collections Repository, the definition of local digital curation principles that we are using has expanded and evolved to encompass not only intellectual curation, but issues of standards and preservation that are enforced through best practices and systems architecture.[2] Digital curation, as we define it, is the ongoing creation of a collection that supports our community's teaching and research, a collection that we add value to, manage, and preserve not just for its current use, but for future scholarly uses and technologies that we have not yet even imagined.

The current UVa Library Digital Collections Repository collections consist of digital images, electronic texts (TEI transcriptions and/or page images), and EAD finding aids that are in transition from their current system. Digital video, audio, datasets, and GIS are part of the Library's collections, and migration of those formats into the managed Repository is in the planning stages. Many of the collections come from over a decade of internal digital production, the creation of surrogates of the Library's physical collections. Some are licensed from vendors. Some are born-digital scholarship created by faculty, often integrating Library materials. Some come from open access sources, such as Federal and state datasets. All of these objects, when brought into the Repository, bring relationships with them, whether simple relationships between media files and metadata, more complex relationships, such as that of page images to a text volume transcription or the relationships between issues of a newspaper, or still more complex relationships, such as the organizational context that a scholar overlays onto a digital archive in a web site. Complex digital scholarly projects are becoming the norm, many of them representing the scope and scale of effort usually spent on writing books. In the future this will become even more complex, as projects that are created around content in the collections are themselves included in the collections, adding new content and relationships and becoming Library material for the next generation of scholars. The digital library must be ready to support these multiple relationships without prejudice to any one context. Curation of objects and their relationships must be part of a Repository.

Digital curation is the creation of a viable social and technical infrastructure for managing and preserving valuable data without significant loss or degradation (Digital Curation Centre, 2005; Hank, 2006). The ultimate aim of our digital curation efforts is to enable the long-term use of the objects in our collections. If an object cannot be discovered, authenticated, rendered, and used, it has not been preserved. Drawing upon our experiences and those of other repositories, we have produced a number of principles of digital curation that we consider vital to the long-term utility and preservation of digital objects. This chapter defines those principles, charts our experience applying them, analyzes their relationship to the success of our Repository efforts, and establishes their broader relevance to other digital libraries.

PRINCIPLES FOR SELECTION OF THE COLLECTIONS

Support teaching and research. This must be our primary principle of digital curation, or we will be building repositories of limited utility. Collections may be selected for their value in the study of a subject in conjunction with the exploration of issues in working with various formats. Faculty in the sciences are now teaching with images, faculty in history are teaching with video, and faculty in English are building data sets. At UVa, subject librarians identify content that supports the curricular and research needs of the community. This content can be born-digital scholarship, existing digital surrogates of physical materials, or physical materials to be digitized. This intellectual curation, where subject librarians apply the same collection analysis and selection criteria as they do for the print and serial collections in addition to facilitating direct requests from faculty, ensures that repository contents serve the teaching and research needs of our community. This is not to say that institutional repositories built through self-deposit are not equally valuable as venues for preservation and open access to published scholarship. Rather, such efforts should be augmented with repositories that select and preserve digital collections used for teaching and research and created as born-digital scholarship rather than as articles or books. All repositories can benefit from this balance of approaches where collections are built through self-deposit, faculty request, and specialist selection.

Promote and improve access to unique and rare items. In prioritizing content to prepare and add to a repository, one of the most important criteria applied after a subject review is that the content is rare or unique to the institution. Journals are increasingly moving to electronic format and digitizing their back files. Mass digitization projects will gradually make their way through published materials held by large research libraries and museums. The preservation digitization of published works will be recorded in registries such as the Digital Library Federation/OCLC Registry of Digital Masters, so local duplication will become less likely as institutions increase awareness of their digitization efforts.[3] The most logical use of localized digitization resources is to focus efforts on rare and uniquely held materials, published or unpublished, including images, works of art, maps, datasets, film or video, recorded sound, printed music, manuscripts, broadsides, and pamphlets not currently included in current mass digitization efforts. For example, with our text collections now being digitized as part of the Google Book Search project, our digitization resources are focusing on the Gordon collection of French Renaissance books, Frances Benjamin Johnston photographs of Virginia architecture, and all the printed music in our Special Collections. The greatest gain for the academic community will come from many institutions focusing their efforts in this manner. This increased availability and visibility of primary materials will improve scholarly research and communication internationally.

Look for value-added possibilities when selecting material to be digitized. At the most basic level, digitization and online availability provide added value through broad dissemination and distributed, unmediated access to anyone with an Internet connection in any location. But there is not enough of a return on investment to warrant the human and equipment resources needed for digitization. One strategy to set a regular production queue into place is to identify high-use content (most often with high circulation numbers or paging requests) that will gain value by digitization, such as enabling full-text searching of an encyclopedia or newspaper. UVa has created a Framework for Digitization that identifies criteria for an ongoing production queue as part of collection building.[4]

Greater value can be added to objects in a repository through the resolution of the digitization or the level of encoding. Digitizing an image to the highest resolution attainable potentially supports more fine-grained examination than may even be possible in the handling of the original. While Optical Character Recognition (OCR) creates full-text access where there was none, creating the most granular structured markup possible of a text using something like the Text Encoding Initiative guidelines improves that full text access and enables the use of analytical tools.[5] Value can also be added through the creation or enrichment of metadata. As an example, special collections might be described only in a general sense in a finding aid or a collection-level catalog record; providing richer metadata indexed as part of a larger set of digital collections almost certainly improves the findability and therefore visibility of primary materials, digital resources, and scholarship at the institution. In the UVa Repository, all formats are indexed together supporting serendipitous discovery across all content types.

Preservation of the physical is a selection criterion for the digital. Library staff regularly identifies physical collections with condition issues or that are at risk for damage, such as brittle books, scores, video or audio, as well as physical formats at risk because the technology needed to access them has become obsolete. An ongoing production queue can be populated with text volumes, brittle scores, and older media formats that have been digitized as part of a preservation reformatting strategy. The incorporation of preservation reformatting projects into production for a repository ensures the continued use of at-risk collections. Brittle tapes of music performances at UVa have recently been reformatted into digital files and will be among the first audio collections added to the Repository. UVa is also reviewing workflows through which brittle books that are digitized during a preservation photocopying process will be integrated into the digital collections.

This principle also extends to collections created in digital formats facing a different sense of brittleness – where the media used to store the files is at risk for damage or corruption, or the hardware or software needed to read the files is no longer readily available. These collections are at risk to the same degree as physical materials. For example, in the migration of UVa's Early American Fiction project from the general Etext collection into the Repository, page images captured as recently as six or eight years ago were found to be unrecoverable due to unreadable CD media or unusable due to write errors in the creation of the CDs.

PRINCIPLES FOR THE USE OF STANDARDS

Preservation of the digital is one of the ultimate goals, but underneath that goal is a standards issue. Sustainable digital preservation strategies require standards, as reliance on standards lessens the threat of format obsolescence in a digital collection. Standards must be selected to embody the best overall compromise between preservability and functionality, and are applied not only in the creation of new collections but in the migration of legacy collections. The UVa Library has gradually developed an inventory of its digital assets created over fifteen years that are candidates for migration into the managed environment of its Repository. The Library is also working with faculty in a "Sustaining Digital Scholarship" initiative to identify seminal works of digital scholarship at UVa that are candidates for migration and collection. Such complex works of digital scholarship such as the Rossetti Archive[6] or the Tibetan and

Himalayan Digital Library[7] can be at-risk due to lack of managed storage, lack of metadata, use of non-standard or proprietary formats, changes in personnel, etc.

The intellectual selection of all materials for the Repository is balanced with a technical assessment, where the materials are compared to an institution's standards, assessed for migration to those standards, and appraised for viability and preservation over time if a full migration is not an option. A migration plan for collection and presentation must be developed for each digital collection, no matter how simple (a set of jpegs) or complex (a structured web site) the collection is. While analysis techniques are similar for all collections, the migration work naturally varies every time, including hand-edited or programmatic normalization and enrichment of metadata, transformation to XML and between DTDs or encoding practices, transformation of media formats, and creation of standardized deliverables.

Enforcement of standards and best practices creates a more controlled environment for preservation. With a controlled set of standards and object classes, an institution has fewer types of files to manage, deliver, and preserve and also limits the scope of future format migrations. The UVa Library identified descriptive, administrative, and structural metadata[8] as well as media format standards[9] and content models[10] (Fedora object classes), and has begun to migrate content to meet those standards as closely as possible to improve the ability to manage, preserve, and deliver the materials. Variation is allowed for legacy collections, including low quality versus high quality images, electronic texts with or without transcriptions or pages images, video with or without transcriptions, etc. An institution must ensure that its standards are in line with those used across the digital library community to enable interoperability where possible (NISO, 2004). There is strong desire and need for an environment where data resources are interoperable, easily discovered, and with appropriate appraisal mechanisms in place for the selection of resources by searchers. The use of common standards and open standards is vital for this interoperability.

PRINCIPLES FOR TRUSTWORTHINESS

The users must be able to trust the objects in the Repository. How does a user determine if an object is trustworthy (Smith, 2003)? Is a transcribed text or OCR the same object as a page image version? How was the text created and could the text have been altered in the process of human markup and error correction? Are the colors accurate in the digitized surrogate of a painting, when the digital surrogate was likely made from an intermediary format, such as a slide or a book? Who validates that the metadata is accurate? An institution's role in the selection, production, documentation, and management of the digital objects in its repository provides a perception of trustworthiness; we have heard as much from our faculty. Requiring minimum standards in the descriptive administrative metadata not only improves the findability of our collections across formats, it also increases the trust level of our objects by documenting their provenance, content, and their digitization process.

Persistence of objects and links to the objects is also an aspect of trustworthiness. As an example, object citations provided by the UVa Repository include persistent URLs. Versioning is also enabled in the Repository – the citations include a generic URL that points to the current version of the object, but there is also a versioned URL so a user can cite and point to the version of the object that he or she viewed at a particular date and time, as an object may be updated in the future.

Appropriate authentication, authorization, rights management and security are not just aspects of the architecture; they are part of the establishment of trust. We are all familiar with the need to secure our servers and authenticate our users. While this is common sense as well as a requirement of many of our licenses, this also helps users to perceive our infrastructure(s) as a trusted environment. In addition, persistent identifiers are necessary to ensure referential integrity over time, and object datastreams must be validated against their purported media formats, using tools such as JHOVE.[11] Digital signatures or checksums must be part of a repository SIP (Submission Information Package, as per the Reference Model for an Open Archival Information System [OAIS]) to ensure that the objects are valid and unchanged over time (ISO, 2002; Kaczmarek et al, 2006). Institutions must strive to document all objects as consistently as possible, meeting descriptive and administrative minimum metadata standards. All rights must be documented – copyright, access restrictions, and use rights – for all objects in both human-readable and machine-actionable formats. Those rights must be translated to access policies which must be enforced through a repository management and delivery infrastructure. The UVa Library has created workflows and a repository architecture based on Fedora (Johnston, 2004).

PRINCIPLES FOR PRESERVATION AND SUSTAINABILITY

Enable the use and sustainability of the Repository collections. Collections of lasting value are both useable and reusable, having the ability to be overlaid in various ways, becoming part of a new array of digital scholarship. The collections must also be sustainable whether comprised of simple media objects, complex objects, or large-scale digital scholarly projects. We are working to identify levels of sustainability that UVa can promise for various types of objects, the functionality that accompanies or is expressed by those objects, and look-and-feel of complex digital projects. Levels of sustainability can best be thought of as a matrix with one set of values determined by the formats and the other set determined by the degree to which available technology can sustain and deliver those formats. This effort goes hand-in-hand with the identification of the controlled set of formats that can be managed, and the ability to migrate objects to meet those format and metadata standards. The further removed from those standards that the objects are, the less likely it is possible to preserve them and their functionality. As well, circumscribing the formats and normalizing metadata provide a controlled environment where one could create elaborate discovery indexes, delivery mechanisms, and tools for the creation of personal collections, slide show, and web sites. It is difficult to say what percentages of objects will be associated with any particular level of sustainability, as this is directly related to our ability to transform legacy materials and create new collections and contexts in a consistent manner. Standards must be well documented for internal production, and documentation and consulting must be made available to faculty for their projects.

Many institutions are thinking not only of the sustainability of media objects, but of the contexts created to organize, annotate, and deliver those objects. This can be accomplished with a flexible, granular approach to managing data as objects with multiple relationships. This must be enabled at a core object architecture level – objects are not monolithic, and their components can be part of multiple contexts and can be added into new contexts by the librarians and scholars who work with them. As an example, in the UVa object architecture a manuscript is an object (a work object), but every page image that makes up that manuscript is also an object (a media object) that can be part of the manuscript's context and part of other contexts, such as a collection of architectural drawings (an aggregation object). In such an architecture, objects are essentially free agents, true to their original contexts but not solely bound to them. UVa has the beginnings of an authoring environment on top of the collections that is capable of taking advantage of not only the objects but the relationships between them, building a new network of contexts and relationships that we will want to collect and preserve on top of the original objects.

Collections should be coupled with tools that support the use of them, such as tools to create personal portfolios of objects, to analyze texts, to tag and annotate objects, to generate slideshows or web pages, and to otherwise author shared digital work. The UVa Library created the Collectus digital object collector tool, which allows users to save personal collections of images and texts from the Repository, generate web pages and slide shows, and manipulate images on-the-fly. Collectus is a generalizable tool for any type of repositories – for example, it was integrated into a proof-of-concept project for the Digital Library Federation's Aquifer (Chavez, Cole, Foulonneau, Habing, Dunn, Parod, and Staples, 2006). Collections are made more usable with tools that support gathering, organization, and transformation of the collections into new forms of scholarly output.

Build a trusted digital repository architecture. Inherently fragile digital objects are more likely to persist over time within a centralized and managed Repository than in a distributed server environment in which levels of server and data management may vary. The development of a repository's architecture should follow the guidelines of the OAIS reference model for trusted repositories. A repository architecture runs in a managed server environment and must validate objects and enforce rights through programmatic rights policies. It is expected that as the range of media formats that we manage increases, we will need to introduce representation format registries into our operations.[12] The UVa Digital Collections Repository manages the delivery versions of our digital resources, and all the metadata about them, including basic representation information, and all the computer programs needed for representation or rendering for the user. We use a system of persistent identifiers for all files in the Repository, which includes changing references to external files that are embedded in XML files or in databases. These core trusted repository architecture attributes are key components in assuring our community that they can trust a repository and that the digital scholarship that we collect will be properly managed and preserved.

Governance and operational policies are of equal importance to standards and architecture. Institutions must develop documented mission statements, policies, and workflows for the operation of their repositories. Policies must include those that ensure the continued review and updating of the standards, workflows, functionality, and the policies themselves. Operational activities must include regular reviews of the operational status, and a periodic audit of the content managed by the repository. Communicating these policies to all stakeholders and keeping them informed of all changes is also a vital part of governance and operations. Perhaps the most challenging task for all institutions will be ensuring that there is organizational support for the operations and a long-term commitment to the service, including budget resources, appropriately skilled staffing, and an adequate technical infrastructure to support the level of activity.

CONCLUSION

How did these principles help the UVa Library? UVa outlined a collection development policy and digitization guidelines to build collections that increase access and use of our unique materials and provide faculty with what they want and need. UVa has identified a set of circumscribed formats and minimum metadata standards to which all objects must adhere. We have a controlled environment that, in theory, simplifies our preservation tasks by minimizing the classes of objects that we must sustain. There is a scaleable architecture with which to manage objects and the relationships among them, operating in a consistent, managed environment that makes the task easier to build discovery and delivery services, and tools for the use of the objects. The collections, services, and tools have been tested by our faculty and we have heard that we are giving them what they want – persistent, trusted collections that contain content that they find useful in their teaching and research, and the tools that they need to use them.

How do these principles more generally guide success and sustainability? The success of a repository can only be assessed against the purpose that the repository serves in its operating environment; no repository can be rated as successful unless it fulfills its purpose. The principles of digital curation set out above can be used to define the environment and the purpose of a repository. They can guide the definition of the scope of a repository, specify the need for a set of circumscribed formats and minimum metadata standards to which objects must adhere, and require the building of a trusted and controlled environment that can simplify preservation tasks and make it easier to build services and tools for the use of the collections. These are the foundations for a sustainable collection.

The ultimate measure of the success of a repository is its ability to sustain access to digital items, but the repository itself also has to be sustainable.[13] Appropriate scope, support, management, and integration into an institution's mission and overall operations are as equally important as the technical infrastructure. The infrastructure of sustainability is both social and technical, something that must be embedded in the culture of our institutions both in the management of our digital collections and as an integral part of new digitization projects. These principles of digital curation set out guidelines for developing policies, standards, and operations that can inform the creation of such an infrastructure, which is the foundation of a sustainable repository service.

NOTES

1. Information about Fedora and its architecture is available at: http://www.fedora.info/.
2. While much is made of the complex issues surrounding digital preservation in the larger discussion of digital curation, intellectual curation and digital preservation are both represented in our curatorial and operational assumptions.
3. For information on the DLF/OCLC Registry of Digital Masters, see <http://www.oclc.org/digitalpreservation/why/digitalregistry/>.
4. The UVa Library Framework for Digitization is available at <http://www.lib.virginia.edu/digital/reports/framework_digitization.html>
5. Information about the Text Encoding Initiative (TEI) is available at <http://www.tei-c.org/>.
6. The Rossetti Archive is available at <http://www.rossettiarchive.org/>.
7. The Tibetan and Himalayan Digital Library is available at <http://www.thdl.org/>.
8. Information about the UVa Library metadata standards is available at <http://www.lib.virginia.edu/digital/metadata/>.
9. Documentation of the UVa Library Internal Production Digitization Standards is available at

<http://www.lib.virginia.edu/digital/reports/uvalib_production_stand ards.htm>.

10. Documentation of the University of Virginia Library Content Models is available at <http://www.lib.virginia.edu/digital/reports/content_models.htm>.

11. For more information, see: JHOVE - JSTOR/Harvard Object Validation Environment http://hul.harvard.edu/jhove/

12. Current representation information and file format registry projects include PRONOM <http://www.records.pro.gov.uk/pronom/>, the Global Digital Format Registry (GDFR) <http://hul.harvard.edu/gdfr/>, and the Presidential Electronic Records Project Operational System (PERPOS) <http://perpos.gtri.gatech.edu/>.

13. There is an increasing role for distributed archiving and preservation systems in addition to local trusted repositories to improve sustainability of digital collections and to ward off catastrophic losses. Key initiatives and organizations include National Digital Information Infrastructure and Preservation Program (NDIIPP) <http://www.digitalpreservation.gov/>, Digital Archiving and Long-Term Preservation (DIGARCH) <http://www.nsf.gov/pubs/2004/nsf04592/nsf04592.htm>, Digital Preservation Coalition <http://www.dpconline.org/>, Digital Curation Centre <http://www.dcc.ac.uk/>, LOCKSS (Lots of Copies Keep Stuff Safe) <http://www.lockss.org/>, and the DELOS digital preservation cluster <http://www.dpc.delos.info/>.

REFERENCES CITED

Chavez, Robert, Timothy W. Cole, Muriel Foulonneau, Thomas G. Habing, Jon Dunn, William Parod, and Thornton Staples. 2006. DLF-Aquifer asset actions experiment: Demonstrating value of actionable URLs. *D-Lib Magazine* 12, no. 10. http://www.dlib.org/dlib/october06/cole/10cole.html.

Digital Curation Centre. 2005. Digital curation and preservation: Defining the research agenda for the next decade, *Report of the Warwick Workshop 7/8 November 2005*. http://www.dcc.ac.uk/training/warwick_2005/Warwick_Workshop_r eport.pdf.

Hank, Carolyn. 2006. Digital curation and institutional repositories: Seeking success. *D-Lib Magazine* 12, no. 7/8. http://www.dlib.org/dlib/july06/hank/07hank.html.

International Standards Organization. 2002. *Reference model for an Open Archival Information System (OAIS)*. Washington, DC: CCSDS. http://public.ccsds.org/publications/archive/650x0b1.pdf.

Johnston, Leslie. 2004. An overview of digital library repository development at the University of Virginia Library. *OCLC Systems & Services: International Digital Library Perspectives* 20, no. 4: 170-173.

---. 2005. Development and assessment of a public discovery and delivery interface for a Fedora repository. *D-Lib Magazine* 11, no. 10. http://www.dlib.org/dlib/october05/johnston/10johnston.html.

Kaczmarek, Joanne, Patricia Hswe, Janet Eke, and Tom Habing. 2006. Using the "Audit checklist of the certification of a trusted digital repository" as a framework for evaluating repository software applications: A progress report. *D-Lib Magazine* 12, no. 12. http://www.dlib.org/dlib/december06/kaczmarek/12kaczmarek.html.

Lagoze, Carl, Sandy Payette, Edwin Shin, and Chris Wilper. 2006. Fedora: An architecture for complex objects and their relationships. *Journal of Digital Libraries, Special Issue on Complex Objects* 6, no. 2: 124-138.

NISO Framework Advisory Group. 2004. *A framework of guidance for building good digital collections. 2nd edition.* Bethesda: National Information Standards Organization. http://www.niso.org/framework/framework2.html.

Smith, Abby. 2003. Authenticity and affect: When is a watch not a watch? *Library Trends* 52: 172-182.

When the Music's Over

Mary Marlino,[1] Tamara Sumner,[1,2] Karon Kelly,[1] and Michael Wright[1]
([1]University Corporation for Atmospheric Research)
([2]University of Colorado at Boulder)

Abstract: Sustaining open access educational digital libraries presents unique challenges and opportunities. This chapter describes these challenges and opportunities, and presents the processes and strategies that were developed to address them at the Digital Library for Earth System Education (DLESE). The authors reflect on their experiences and highlight which of these processes and strategies may be applicable to other digital library sustainability efforts.

INTRODUCTION

For the past seven years we have been operating the Digital Library for Earth System Education (DLESE – www.dlese.org), with generous funding from the Geoscience Directorate of the National Science Foundation (NSF). Like all good things, grants from the NSF end at some point; in DLESE's case, in Fall 2007. We have been tasked with developing and implementing a sustainability plan that will ensure that DLESE users will continue to have open access to the educational resources and collections in the library for the "foreseeable future."

DLESE is a large, geoscience education community undertaking involving scientists, educators, and library builders from many institutions across the nation. The goal of this grassroots, community-led project is to provide searchable access to high-quality, online educational resources for K-12 and undergraduate Earth system science education (Marlino et al., 2001). These resources include simulations, maps, lesson plans, lab exercises, data sets, virtual field trips, and interactive demonstrations. As leaders of the DLESE Program Center (DPC) at the University Corporation for Atmospheric Research (UCAR), we were charged with developing and operating the library's core technical infrastructure, accessioning and maintaining collections, supporting library use in educational settings, supporting the library's community governance processes, and ensuring program continuity across the distributed technology and collection building efforts.

Sustaining open access educational digital libraries, particularly those based on distributed development models, presents unique challenges and opportunities. In this chapter, we will briefly describe these challenges and opportunities, and present the processes and strategies that we developed to address them. We reflect on our experiences to date to highlight which of these processes and strategies may be applicable to other digital library sustainability efforts. These reflections stem from experiences and perspectives at the DPC, and are not intended to represent the full breadth and depth of the DLESE experience.

THE DIGITAL LIBRARY FOR EARTH SYSTEM EDUCATION

The NSF conceived of DLESE as a bold experiment to promote and embody the vision for geoscience education reform: promoting teaching about the Earth as a complex system, integrating research and education, supporting inquiry learning and the "doing of science" by K-16 learners, and promoting the use of Earth science data in the classroom. The vision for DLESE was born out of a broad-based community workshop, "Portal to the Future," held in the summer of 1999 (Manduca & Mogk, 1999). This workshop brought together 50 thought leaders from different disciplines within the geosciences; e.g., atmospheric, solid Earth, ocean science, etc. These participants had little to no prior experience working together, few had any digital library experience, and there was little common agreement on what it meant to teach about the Earth as a system. In 1999, both the Earth "systems" perspective and digital library technologies were nascent. However, Portals workshop participants shared enthusiasm about the promise of the new geoscience education agenda, a commitment to work together to build a digital library, and an excitement about the potential of DLESE as a major vehicle for education reform.

While the users of DLESE were potentially all educators and learners interested in Earth science, to make building the library tractable, development was structured into three distinct versions targeting different user groups. Version 1 focused on supporting early adopters and library builders within the geoscience community; Version 2 focused on supporting mainstream K-16 educators; and Version 3 was intended to support students and the general public. Version 3 was originally planned for a 2007 roll-out but was eliminated to allow us to focus on sustainability planning instead. Thus, Version 2 is the focus of our sustainability efforts. Figure 7.1 shows the current library interface.

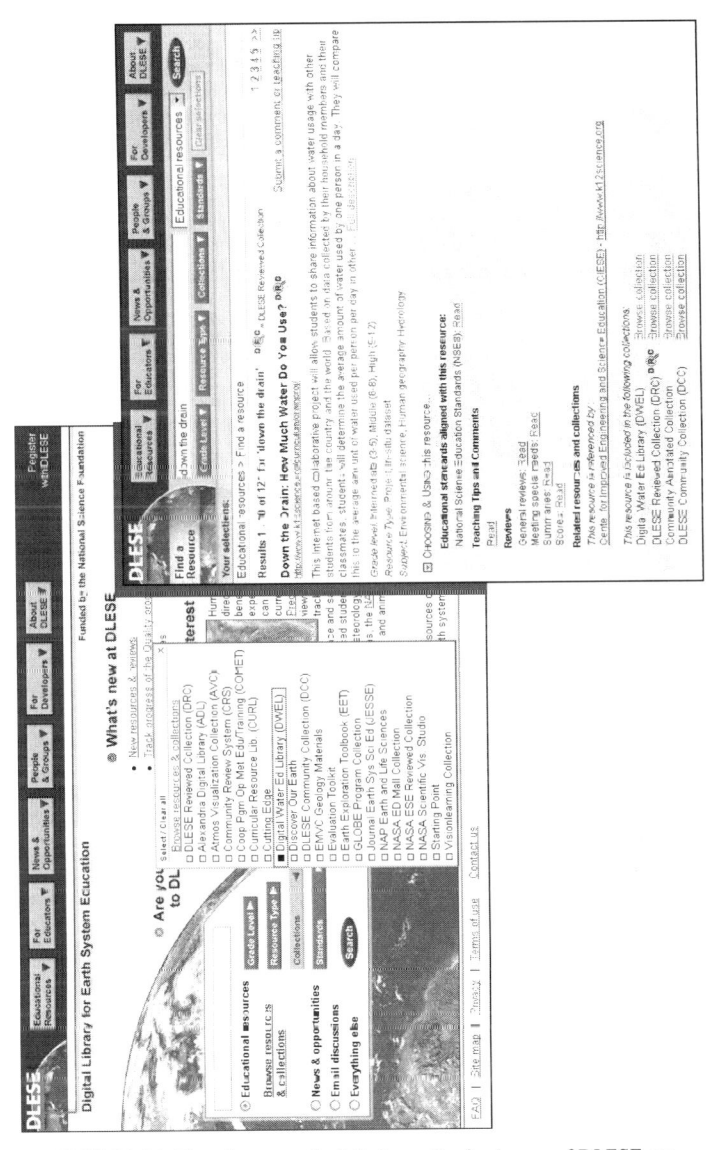

FIGURE 6.1: The picture on the left shows the front page of DLESE.org. Users can search for educational resources using keywords or criteria such as grade level, resource type, and educational standards. The pop-up lists the individual collections that are in the library. The picture on the right shows a typical search results page, where the "Choose and Use" option has been selected. This option provides educationally useful contextual information about a resource such as standards information and reviews.

The primary capabilities and content embodied in this version include:

- Access to approximately 13,500 digital educational resources, organized into 41 thematic collections contributed by 25 different institutions. Thematic collections fall into two general categories: those created by scientific organizations such as NASA to organize and disseminate resources developed in-house, and those developed by third-party aggregators. Resources in the library were created by a wide variety of individual faculty members, agencies, and institutions and are held (stored) on local servers. Users access resources through the library via searchable metadata records that describe and/or annotate them. Resources in DLESE are described using a metadata framework based on IEEE-LOM that supports rich educational descriptions, including a wide variety of K-12 science and math education standards, and geospatial and temporal descriptions (http://www.dlese.org/Metadata/). Collections in DLESE are also made available to the National Science Digital Library (NSDL) and DLESE serves as the de facto geoscience "node" in the NSDL network of libraries.

- Tools to support collection development and curation. The DLESE Collection System (DCS) enables collection developers to catalog educational resources (lesson plans, modules, data, imagery, etc.), news and opportunities announcements, and annotations about resources. The DCS can support any metadata framework described in XML schema, enabling the tool to flexibly and dynamically adapt to new or modified metadata frameworks without requiring additional programming effort. The tool includes an Open Archives Initiative Protocol for Metadata Harvesting (OAI-PMH) data provider that allows collections and metadata managed within the system to be easily shared. We are currently extending the Digital Collection System to use the NSDL Data Repository to enable NSDL libraries to manage collections in this Fedora-based repository (http://fedoraproject.org/index.html).

- A sophisticated discovery service, supporting both searching and browsing, based on the Lucene engine (Weatherley, 2004). Users can search DLESE collections by keyword, grade-level, educational resource type, and educational standard. Library developers can embed this search service into their own libraries and portals using a public web service protocol, which supports all of the above capabilities as well as searching by geo-spatial footprints (ibid). This service was adapted by NSDL for use in the NSDL search service.

- A variety of mechanisms for user contributions, including a "Suggest a Resource" feature, a community review system enabling both teachers and learners to submit reviews (Kastens, 2001), and a facility for submitting teaching tips and other informal comments.

- Several forms of support for community building including a News and Opportunities service, hosting of listservs for geoscience education groups, and a community newsletter called DLESE Matters. Earlier versions of the library included hosting of collaboration tools such as wikis and plones for both distributed library builders and geoscience education groups.

- A technical infrastructure supporting all of these capabilities based on open platforms and open standards, e.g., Lucene, OAI-PMH, java, and javascript, which can be downloaded from SourceForge.net. Major components of this infrastructure were developed and operated by the DLESE Program Center, while others were developed and operated by groups at Columbia University and Carleton College.

- An active and significant user base, exceeding over a million library sessions annually. Surveys reveal that over 60% of these users are K-12 teachers and students, with the remaining groups spread out among higher education, general public, and other library developers.

A distinguishing feature of DLESE from the beginning was its emphasis on community involvement and governance in all aspects of library building and operations. One outcome of the Portals workshop was the DLESE Community Plan (Manduca & Mogk, 2000), which laid out a framework for governance and a committee structure for the library. This framework called for a 12-member Steering Committee and four Standing Committees for Technology, Users, Services, and Collections. Thus, there was significant community input into all library policies and the concomitant design of library processes based on these policies. Given the emphasis on supporting community engagement, policies tended to emphasize "high touch" approaches over automation in order to ensure inclusiveness and diversity in library building. In 2003, NSF expanded upon this community governance structure by funding four additional DLESE Centers – Community, Collections, Evaluation, and Data – distributed throughout the country. In 2005, NSF added an additional management entity – the DLESE Project Office – to coordinate and manage the activities of the five distributed Centers. At the end of 2005, NSF made the decision to discontinue funding for the distributed library centers and the DLESE Program Office. In FY 2006, the DLESE Program Center received a final year of funding to continue support for library infrastructure, support for community collection developers, service to library users, and to develop a library sustainability plan.

SUSTAINABILITY PLANNING

We were asked by NSF to develop a sustainability plan that would:

- Continue to make all DLESE resources widely available for the purpose of education
- Acknowledge NSF support for the initial development of DLESE in all future publications
- Honor the DLESE Intellectual Property Policy established July 2, 2002, the essential element being that the IP for metadata or technologies created by community members for the library would remain the property of their home institution.

In addition, NSF asked us to convene an advisory board to provide guidance on sustainability planning, criteria for decision-making and selection of new business models or host environments, and recommendations for new hosts. This board was composed of recognized experts in geoscience, library operations and strategic planning, and business.

To develop this plan, we went through a structured analysis process consisting of the following major steps, as elaborated below:

- Defining core library components and determining what should be sustained

- Developing a taxonomy characterizing different operational levels
- Developing cost estimates for different operational levels
- Developing criteria for selecting new business models or host environments
- Developing a range of models characterizing different hosting configurations
- Conducting an IP audit

Defining core library components and determining what should be sustained

A key challenge in sustainability planning is disaggregating components of the library and determining what should be sustained. This is a complex issue with no single correct answer. Digital libraries have many different, yet interdependent, components such as content, technology infrastructure, and end-user services. In this process, we defined the components of library operations to include system administration, application support, content processes, workflows, maintenance, and use metrics. "Content" refers to the development and curation of collections, educational resources, and the library portal website. We defined library services as those providing support for library developers and end-users, including customer support for tools, collections building, and resource use. We recognized that sustainability would depend on simplifying processes and workflows in all three of these areas.

Developing a taxonomy characterizing different operational levels

After determining the core content, infrastructure, and services that should be sustained, we recognized that different configurations of these library components would place different demands on the host environments. Working with the NSF and our Advisory Board, we developed a taxonomy characterizing four levels of service reflecting different levels of demands on the host environment.

Level 1 Service, the minimum required by NSF, is characterized by offering access to library collections as static HTML pages available on the Web. That is, each item-level metadata record in the library would be rendered as a web page and users would access the DLESE collections directly through their web browsers or via commercial search engines. This level requires a host environment to provide web site hosting only, and satisfies the NSF mandate of preserving open access to collections for educational purposes. In this service level, we envision that the quality of the user experience would be significantly compromised, since library services such as searching and browsing would no longer be available, and resources in library collections would increasingly become unavailable and outdated since collections would not be actively curated.

Level 2 Service focuses solely on sustaining library content; i.e., the metadata records describing resources and collections. This level is characterized by providing users with access to DLESE collections through a third party site, such as a university or public library. In this level, metadata records would be ingested into the collection management systems already in place in the host environment. Access to DLESE collections would be provided through existing end-user interfaces such as online library catalogs. Curation of DLESE collections would be performed using whatever tools and processes are already in place. This level requires a host environment to provide collection curation services only, and places no new technical demands on potential hosts. In this service level, what is potentially lost is the significant user-base of DLESE. It is unlikely the teachers and students would successfully find DLESE collections once they are embedded into larger and more diverse library holdings.

Level 3 Service is the continuation of current library operations and selected end-user services. That is, users access curated collections and services through the interface at DLESE.org. In addition to searching and accessing library collections, DLESE would continue to offer services such as Resource of the Month (featuring a selected learning resource on the front page), the DLESE Matters community newsletter, and a news and opportunities service featuring internships, summer research, conferences, and job opportunities within the geosciences. This level requires a host environment to provide technical hosting for both hardware and software systems, collection curation, and support for selected library services. In this service level, the transition to a new host should be largely transparent to end-users as their core services remain intact. What would be potentially lost at this level are services and supports that DLESE historically provided to the broader geoscience community and to library developers. For instance, services such as hosting of community listservs and accessioning of new collections on demand as they become available would all be discontinued. In addition, there would be a reduced service level for some of the continued services. For instance, the newsletter would be published quarterly rather than monthly, and the news and opportunities would not be updated as frequently. Maintaining these services at the historically provided service levels would place significant demands on a host environment in terms of ongoing human effort.

Level 4 Service is based on modifying library systems to achieve significant integration with the NSDL technical infrastructure, specifically the NSDL Data Repository released in early 2007. This Fedora-based infrastructure is operated by NSDL on behalf of its community and it currently provides reliable technical operations at no additional cost to NSDL member libraries.

From a user and library perspective, this level supports Level 3 services and also preserves the integration of DLESE collections into NSDL. Additionally, discontinued community services such as collaboration tools would now be available through NSDL for host environment use. In this service level, the host environment would still be responsible for collection curation and end-user support. However, the demands and costs of technical hosting and software maintenance would be significantly reduced as these activities are performed by NSDL.

Developing cost estimates for different operational levels

The primary challenge that we faced in developing reasonable cost estimates for future operations is that any reliable estimate is completely dependent upon the new host's technical and human resource infrastructure, as well as the level of service to be provided. The potential range of estimates, therefore, is quite varied. Given these uncertainties, we decided to parse out the major functions that would have to be undertaken to guarantee Level 3 Service, and base our estimates on what this level of sustainability would approximately cost with our existing institutional infrastructure and talent base intact. We operated on the assumption that in order to maintain DLESE's currency, and therefore its relevancy to users, library content would continue to grow at a modest pace, requiring the services of staff for library curation procedures. Library services, specifically periodic updates and occasional bug fixes, are anticipated to require some minimal level of software engineer service. Finally, some modest level of administrative support will be required for general administrative and community support functions. We also assumed that the costs associated with technical hosting of hardware and software would be absorbed into the current operations of the new hosts as part of their larger operations and thus did not include direct charges for this in our costs estimates. Based on these assumptions, we estimate that the annual cost of continuing uninterrupted basic DLESE operations to be approximately one tenth of annual DLESE operating expenses during those years when DLESE was fully functioning as a distributed community library.

One tenth is a huge cost savings over previous operational models. To achieve this savings, previous DLESE functions, such as its committee structure and community governance, the distributed construction processes, and the significant effort that went into community building and outreach have all been eliminated from the model. In addition to the significant cost savings that these measures permitted, we have made a considerable effort over the past year to streamline the operational costs associated with DLESE, including discontinuing support for many community and library developer services, and automating workflows and maintenance procedures around continued end-user and collections services as much as possible.

Developing Criteria for Hosts Selection

The criteria that we developed for selecting a host were based on four factors: the mandates provided by NSF, the legal status, the organizational capabilities, and the financial stability of a potential host environment. The legal status of an organization refers to its ability to assume liability for the DLESE intellectual property, privacy and terms of use policies. As a guiding philosophy, we were committed to honoring the original policies developed by the DLESE community. Given that the library had grown significantly through community contributions made under the auspices of these policies, we believed that maintaining the policies in the new environment would be a key factor in preserving both community trust and the integrity of the various library systems and collections through the transition.

Reliable operations of a digital library such as DLESE require technical skills, library skills, and domain expertise. Necessary organizational capabilities include significant experience with operating and maintaining server hardware and the software systems that underpin library operations, and experience in curating library collections, ideally digital collections where web-based resources are continually monitored for availability. The host organization must also have sufficient knowledge to answer support questions. For DLESE, these questions often require domain knowledge in both geoscience and education.

We felt it was important that potential hosts demonstrate financial commitment and stability that could ensure library operations for at least three years. Ensuring stable library operations for a three year period seemed to be a minimally acceptable "return on investment" for a one year planning effort.

Developing a range of models characterizing different hosting configurations

As we began to consider what types of organizations or organizational configurations would provide a suitable hosting environment for DLESE, and as we proceeded in discussions with various groups that had expressed interest, several models emerged that were helpful to our deliberations:

- *Sponsorship Model.* In this model, DLESE sustainability would be undertaken by an allied Earth science professional society, or a public or government agency. An alternative scenario under this model would be sponsorship through private foundation support. This model does not necessarily assume that the sponsoring agency would be the actual host institution for operational services.

- *Hybrid Model.* This model is a variation of the above, but blends public and private sector support. Again, this model does not assume that the sponsoring agency would be the actual host institution for operational services.

- *Adoption Model.* In this model, an institution (collegiate, private, government, etc.) would subsume DLESE operating costs into an existing budget as part of their institutional remit. That is, the institution would consider the mission of DLESE and its operating requirements to be so closely aligned with its core mission that DLESE would become an additional service that the institution would provide to its stakeholders and core constituencies. An example of this might be in the form of technical hosting services from a group such as the San Diego Supercomputing Center, or curation services from an organization such as the University of Colorado Benson Geology Library or the NCAR Library.

- *Partnership Model.* In this model, multiple organizations or organizational entities in one institution would assume responsibility for different components of library development under a collaborative agreement. An example of this would be a partnership between the National Center for Atmospheric Research (NCAR) Library for curation services, the NCAR Computational and Information Systems Laboratory (CISL) for hosting services, and the University Corporation for Atmospheric Research (UCAR) Office of Programs for system support and upgrades.

Our considerations of these various models indicated that the partnership model was the most promising one for DLESE. In our discussions with potential hosts, we found that very few organizations have the combination of mission alignment and all three capabilities – technical, library, and domain knowledge and skills – in house. Identifying organizations with both capabilities and mission alignment proved to be tricky since DLESE's primary user audience is K-12. For instance, organizations serving this audience often do not have the same level of technical skills or hosting infrastructure as those found in national labs or large universities.

Conducting an IP audit

A key issue related to the transition of DLESE to another host or operator concerns intellectual property rights and ownership of collections and technical infrastructure. UCAR (DLESE's current host institution) owns 45% of the metadata in DLESE, 15% is in the public domain (e.g., NASA data), and the remainder are owned by 22 other institutions. The core infrastructure and technologies for DLESE developed at UCAR will continue to be available on SourceForge under a GPL open source license. One of the lessons learned is that obtaining licenses or permissions related to transfer of intellectual property rights between institutions can be an extended process; negotiations around the transfer of some DLESE technologies developed at a major university took nearly 12 months. The experience of obtaining this license indicates that negotiations with the other 22 institutions owning metadata could be a significant and time-consuming undertaking. As with developing accurate cost estimates, it is not possible to negotiate these remaining IP transfers without knowing who the end-recipient host will be.

REFLECTIONS AND CONSIDERATIONS

It is not often we find opportunities to quote the Doors in the title of an academic article. In this case, we are pleased to report that while the music may be over in terms of significant NSF funding for DLESE, as a result of our sustainability planning, no one is going to be turning out the lights on library operations for the foreseeable future. We have successfully negotiated agreements with UCAR and NCAR who will collaboratively provide the capabilities to continue Level 3 Service; i.e., continue to make DLESE collections and core end-user services available through DLESE.org.

It is a common refrain amongst those discussing sustainability planning to remark that it should be taken into account from the beginning of a project. But what exactly does this mean in terms of day-to-day processes in library development, management, and operations? Our experiences over the past twelve months have prompted the following reflections on this question that may be useful to other programs as they consider their sustainability plans and options.

First, we found it extraordinarily useful to have an advisory board dedicated to sustainability planning. In retrospect, the DLESE effort would have benefited from establishing a separate advisory board focused solely on this challenge early in the project. For future projects and programs, establishing such a board could serve two very useful purposes. It is easy to get swept up in managing day-to-day operations. Sustainability planning often gets relegated to that 'rainy day' that never quite materializes. Having a board that convened twice annually would keep this challenge in the mainstream and ensure that progress was made on this issue from the very beginning. A board focused exclusively on sustainability planning would most likely be very different in composition from a board focusing on how the project could best serve the needs of the diverse community of users. Namely, we would recommend that a sustainability board have members with experience in business and successful track records in sustaining or handing over projects to new institutional homes or business models. Boards focused on serving community needs are often comprised of leaders in the community being served; in our case, members of the geoscience research and education community. In addition to bringing in invaluable forms of expertise, this separate board could fulfill a vital function in providing advice about how to strike a balance between providing community services and controlling costs.

Second, as presaged above, developing a disciplined model for cost control is a critical element for long-term project sustainability. The more expensive day-to-day development and operations are, the more difficult it will be to sustain them in the long-term. For projects built around grant initiatives or community-based governance, cost structures are often not under direct control. For instance, the granting agency may institute a preferred form of management or distributed operations. Likewise, community-based governance processes may decide to enact policies that prioritize high-touch community support over more automated approaches. There is a difficult and delicate tension between building the library and building the community. Both must go hand-in-hand, but in our experience, they have very different cost structures. It is incumbent upon the broader digital library and scientific communities to develop a more detailed and thorough understanding of the cost structures and benefits for different architectures around collaboration and distributed construction, particularly in this era of eScience and eResearch.

Third, critical partnerships with organizations that have the potential to sustain the library must be established at the onset. DLESE's early partnerships were developed primarily to support library development. In retrospect, it would have been extremely helpful to have had more partners early on who were willing to assume responsibility for DLESE, or its components, and to recognize this responsibility as a critical element of the partnership. A promising development is the fact that the NSDL Pathways initiatives have recognized this, and are now actively encouraged to build formal relationships with their relevant professional societies as a vehicle for long-term sustainability.

Finally, we recognize that sustaining the library's community of developers and users is perhaps the most important, albeit most difficult, aspect of library sustainability. One of the most enduring artifacts of the DLESE experience is a community with an enhanced level of digital library expertise, sharing resources for the common good. A frequently cited definition of "sustainability" is the one created by the Brundtland Commission (United Nations, 1987), which defined sustainable development (in this particular case, economic and agricultural development) as development that "meets the needs of the present without compromising the ability of future generations to meet their own needs." This philosophy has guided our planning over the past 12 months as we considered our sustainability options to ensure that our library and our library community remain vibrant and relevant in years to come.

REFERENCES

Kastens, K.A. 2001. How to identify the "best" resources for the reviewed collection of the Digital Library for Earth System Education. Column "Another node on the interNet," *Computers & Geosciences* 27, no. 3: 375-378.

Manduca, Cathryn A. and David W. Mogk. 1999. Portal to the future: A digital library for earth system education. Report from the Portal to the Future Workshop, August 8-11, Berkeley Springs, WV.

---. 2000. The digital library for earth system education (DLESE): A community plan. Report from the University of Oklahoma to the National Science Foundation, Grant 99-06648. http://www.dlese.org/documents/plans/CommPlanFinal_secure.pdf

Marlino, Mary R., Tamara Sumner, David W. Fulker, Cathryn A. Manduca, and David W. Mogk. 2001. The digital library for earth system education (DLESE): Building community, building the library. *Communications of the Association for Computing Machinery (ACM); Special Issue on Digital Libraries* 44, no.5, 80-81.

Weatherley, John. 2004. DLESE search service documentation. http://www.dlese.org/dds/services/ddsws1-1/service_specification.jsp (accessed April 6, 2007).

United Nations. 1987. Report of the World Commission on Environment and Development. General Assembly Resolution 42/187, December 11.

About the Editors and Contributors

Paul Arthur Berkman integrates science, policy and information technology as a Research Professor at the Bren School of Environmental Science & Management at the University of California Santa Barbara. Dr. Berkman also is the CEO and co-founder of EvREsearch LTD, which utilizes its patented Digital Integration System (DigIn®) for government and business applications. In addition, he serves as the Chair of the Sustainability Standing Committee for the National Science Digital Library program. Dr. Berkman completed his M.S. and Ph.D. in oceanography in 1986 and 1988, respectively, at the University of Rhode Island. For his research and education activities Dr. Berkman has received the Antarctic Service Medal from the United States Congress, as well as fellowships from the Japanese Ministry of Science, Education and Culture; National Aeronautics and Space Administration; National Science Foundation; The Ohio State University; and University of Canterbury.

Bradley Daigle is Director of Scholarly Resources, part of the Digital Scholarship Services group at the University of Virginia Library. Previously he was the Project Supervisor for the Virginia Heritage Project—an NEH funded grant. Mr. Daigle is one of the many participants in The University of Virginia's Digital Library program and oversees digital publishing services, digitization services, repository services, and digital collection management. He works with faculty and other strategic partners at The University of Virginia to both support and sustain digital scholarship. He received his MA in literature from the University of Montreal in 1996 and MLS from Catholic University in 1999.

Michael J. Furlough is the Assistant Dean for Scholarly Communications and co-director of the Office of Digital Scholarly Publishing at the Penn State University Libraries. He is responsible for developing and leading the library's scholarly communications program, including the departments of Digitization and Preservation and Scholarly Communications Services. Through the Office of Digital Scholarly Publishing he collaborates with the Penn State Press to develop services and programs leading to alternative channels and business models for supporting informal and peer-reviewed publications. Previously Furlough served as Director of Digital Research and Instructional Services at the

University of Virginia Library, where he gained extensive experience in consulting with scholars in all disciplines on the application of a wide range of technologies to their teaching and research.

Martin Halbert is Director of Digital Programs and Systems at the Emory University Libraries and directs all digital library services and systems functions for the Emory General Libraries. He is responsible for researching and leading library information technology initiatives, including all digital scholarly communication projects of the MetaScholar Initiative (http:// MetaScholar.org). Dr. Halbert provides a leadership role within the library for computer systems operations, development, planning, and integration. He is the principal investigator for research projects with budgets totaling $4.8M. He is the founding President of the Educopia Institute, an independent not-for-profit 501(c)3 educational organization dedicated to improving scholarly communication in socially responsible ways (http://educopia.org). With support from the Library of Congress in 2003, he established the MetaArchive Cooperative, a growing consortium of cultural heritage institutions that provides distributed digital preservation services (http:// MetaArchive.org).

Leslie Johnston is the Head of Digital Publishing Services at the University of Virginia Library, where she manages programs to provide digital scholarly publishing services and deliver and expand access to the University of Virginia's distinctive digital collections and scholarship. Previously, she served as the Head of Instructional Technology and Library Information Systems at the Harvard Design School, as the Academic Technology Specialist for Art for the Stanford University Libraries, and as Database Specialist for the Getty Research Institute. Ms. Johnston has also been active in the museum community, working for various museums, teaching courses on museum systems and digitization, editing the journal *Spectra*, and serving on the board of the Museum Computer Network.

Karon Kelly is Director of Digital Learning Sciences at the University Corporation for Atmospheric Research. She has extensive experience in education and science libraries, with specific expertise in digital library design and development. She is responsible for DLS strategic and operational planning, oversight and development of DLS staff and financial resources and services. Previously she was Deputy Director for the Digital Library for Earth System Education (DLESE) where she oversaw DLESE's information modeling, metadata, and library collection development activities.

Mary Marlino is the Director of e-Science and the National Center for Atmospheric Research (NCAR) Library. Previously, she was a principal investigator and Director of the Digital Library for Earth System Education Program Center, where she led the NSF-funded community development efforts for this geoscience education initiative. Prior to this, Dr. Marlino was the Director of Educational Technology at the United States Air Force Academy. She has significant experience in the management of innovative educational programs and library services and in the evaluation of educational technologies.

Katherine Skinner is the Executive Director of the Educopia Institute, an independent not-for-profit 501(c)3 educational organization dedicated to improving scholarly communication in socially responsible ways (http://educopia.org). Dr. Skinner also serves as Digital Projects Librarian for the Emory University Libraries, providing leadership and strategic direction for the library's digital initiatives that are supported through sponsored funding. She is a Co-Principal Investigator on the SouthComb Cyberinfrastructure for Scholars Project (http://southcomb.org), a founder and editorial board member of *Southern Spaces* (http://southernspaces.org) and manages the MetaArchive Cooperative, a distributed digital preservation service organization supported by the Library of Congress and the National Historical Publications and Records Commission (http://metaarchive.org). She holds a BA from the University of North Carolina at Chapel Hill and a PhD in American Studies from Emory University.

Tamara Sumner is Executive Director of DLS. She is responsible for leadership, strategy development, and the conduct of the DLS research program. Sumner is also an Associate Professor at the University of Colorado, with a joint appointment between the Institute of Cognitive Science and the Department of Computer Science. She has significant experience in the theory, design, and evaluation of interactive learning environments, human-centered systems, digital libraries, and intelligent information systems. Since 2000, she has published over 50 articles on these topics.

Tyler O. Walters is the Associate Director of Technology and Resource Services at the Georgia Institute of Technology Library and Information Center. He provides leadership, vision, and expertise in digital library programs, information technologies, electronic resources management, metadata, and archives and records. Mr. Walters is a co-Principal Investigator with the MetaArchive Cooperative, one of the eight original digital preservation partnerships with the Library of Congress' National Digital Information Infrastructure and Preservation Program (http:// metaarchive.org). His recent committee appointments include the National Science Foundation's National Science Digital Library Sustainability Committee, the Association of College and Research Libraries' Research Committee, and Chair of the DSpace User Group Program Committee for the 2nd International Conference on Open Repositories 2007. Mr. Walters was also a member of the ARL / NSF workgroup that produced the report, *"To Stand the Test of Time: Long term Stewardship of Data Sets in Science and Engineering,"* (http://www.arl.org/bm~doc/digdatarpt.pdf). The author of 20 published articles and presenter at over 50 professional conferences, Mr. Walters is a past recipient of the Society of American Archivists' Ernst Posner Award for best article in the *American Archivist* (1998). He holds a Master of Arts in Library and Information Science from the University of Arizona, a Master of Arts in Archival Management from North Carolina State University, and a B.A. in History from Northern Illinois University.

Michael Wright is the Chief Technical Officer and e-Science Strategist for Digital Learning Sciences. He examines how emerging technologies can enhance the delivery of digital learning services and develops strategies to integrate e-learning and e-Science services with emerging national infrastructures. Previously, he was the technical director of the DLESE Program Center and was responsible for the development and operation of the technical infrastructure of DLESE. Wright has authored numerous publications on advances in scholarly communication and technology-support learning and has received 13 patents for innovative work in the commercial sector.

Made in the USA